The Concise Guide
to
Interpreting Accounts

The Concise Guide
to
Interpreting Accounts

J.D. Blake

Department of Management Studies
Loughborough University of Technology

CHAPMAN & HALL
London · New York · Tokyo · Melbourne · Madras

Published by Chapman & Hall, 2–6 Boundary Row, London SE1 8HN

Chapman & Hall, 2–6 Boundary Row, London SE1 8HN, UK

Chapman & Hall, 29 West 35th Street, New York NY10001, USA

Chapman & Hall Japan, Thomson Publishing Japan, Hirakawacho Nemoto Building, 7F, 1-7-11 Hirakawa-cho, Chiyoda-ku, Tokyo 102, Japan

Chapman & Hall Australia, Thomas Nelson Australia, 102 Dodds Street, South Melbourne, Victoria 3205, Australia

Chapman & Hall India, R. Seshadri, 32 Second Main Road, CIT East, Madras 600 035, India

First edition 1989
Reprinted 1990, 1991

© 1989

Typeset in 10/11 Palatino by Best-set Typesetter Ltd, Hong Kong
Printed in Great Britain by T.J. Press (Padstow) Ltd, Padstow, Cornwall

ISBN   0 412 38280 6

Contents

Acknowledgements   vii
Preface   ix

1   The interpretation of accounts — some key issues   1
2   The assessment of the liquidity position   7
3   Analysing the financial structure   13
4   Analysis of performance   23
5   Investor ratios   31
6   Other tools of interpretation   39
7   Drawing conclusions   43
8   A full example   49

Appendix 1: Accounts of Barchester plc   55
Appendix 2: Accounts of Crosby plc   57
Improving examination performance on financial analysis   63
Questions 1 to 38   65
Suggested solutions to questions 1 to 32   109

Index   159

Acknowledgements

The book aims to serve both the exam candidate and the practitioner. For the exam candidate the book offers a wide-ranging approach designed to meet the demands of all the professional accountancy bodies as well as other professional associations in the finance sector. For the practitioner the book offers a coherent, structured and comprehensive approach to ratio analysis.

The author wishes to thank the following professional bodies for permission to quote from their examination papers. Where an abbreviation has been used in the text when attributing questions, that abbreviation is shown in brackets:

Association of International Accountants (AIA)

Chartered Association of Certified Accountants (when questions from the Certified Diploma in Finance and Accounting have been used the abbreviation Cert.Dip.F.A. is used)

Institute of Bankers (AIB) (now the Chartered Institute of Bankers — CIB)

Institute of Chartered Accountants in England and Wales (ICAEW)

Institute of Chartered Accountants in Ireland (ICAI)

Institute of Chartered Accountants in Scotland (ICAS)

Institute of Cost and Management Accountants (ICMA) (now the Chartered Institute of Management Accountants — CIMA)

Society of Company and Commercial Accountants (SCCA)

In all cases the author is responsible for the solutions printed.

Preface

The art of using accounts involves a thorough understanding of accounting principles, a knowledge of a range of techniques used in interpretation, particularly ratio analysis, and an instinct for identifying problem areas that can only be developed with experience.

This book presents a detailed description of the most commonly used interpretation techniques, and explains how these can be used. It also presents a wide range of interpretation problems, many of them drawn from examination papers of a number of professional bodies. Specimen solutions for most of these questions are also included, but in order to give students an opportunity to work totally unseen exercises, some questions are presented without solutions.

Thus the volume gives the reader the opportunity to gain experience of handling interpretation problems by working each question, and then consulting the solution offered by the author. In this way experience is built up by what is effectively a case-study approach.

1 The interpretation of accounts — some key issues

Introduction

Considerable resources are devoted to the preparation of accounts. In recent years there has been a substantial increase in the quantity of data contained in published accounts as a result of new company law requirements and new Statements of Standard Accounting Practice (SSAPs). The increased detail provided in accounts provides the analyst with the opportunity to delve deeper, but requires greater interpretative skills. In this book we will look in detail at the range of tools available to the analyst.

The importance of user needs

In the interpretation of accounts it is always important to consider in detail the special needs of the user who is being served. For example, short-term creditors of a company will be primarily concerned with an analysis of the current liquidity position, whereas equity shareholders will be more concerned with profitability. All users will have access to the published accounts of a business, such as the accounts filed with the registrar of companies by a limited company. Some users may also have access to further financial data by right or by agreement. For instance, the management of a company will have access to the management accounts, and a bank may require that the business disclose further financial data before agreeing a loan. Some users will also be able to make judgements on the financial position of a business on the basis of their observation of transactions. A supplier who observes that a customer is delaying payment for goods received, for example, may regard this as evidence of liquidity problems. Observations of this kind may lead to further investigation, possibly by reference to the published accounts.

Limitations

The value of any interpretation of accounts exercise is restricted by the deficiencies of the accounts themselves as a tool for decision-making.

Where published accounts are used these will be presented some months after the accounting year end of a business; for example, a private limited company is required to file accounts within ten months of its year end, so that the most recent published accounts may relate to a balance sheet date up to twenty-two months earlier. Moreover, many companies delay submission of their accounts even further, so that the user may be relying on data that are significantly out of date. Published accounts, moreover, present a very limited range of data. For example, depending on which profit and loss account format under the 1985 Companies Act is chosen, a limited company may not disclose the cost of sales.

A problem in the use of all accounts that has worried the accounting profession in recent years is the distorting effect of inflation. When the historical cost convention is followed in times of inflation, the following problems arise:

1. The monetary unit in which the accounts are expressed represents a different measure of value in successive years. For example, an increase in the monetary amount of sales may be shown although the volume of sales may have fallen.
2. Assets consumed are recorded as expenses in the profit and loss account at historical cost, although the cost of replacement may be higher. Therefore it is argued that the profit figure is overstated in terms of the real increase in value obtained by the business.
3. Assets shown in the balance sheet are recorded at historical cost although, as a result of price level changes, their current value may be substantially higher.

The combined effect of overstating profit and understating assets is to distort the ratio of return on capital employed (discussed in detail below).

All accounts are prepared in accordance with accounting policies that in practice can vary substantially from one business to another, with a consequent impact on the reported figures. Where accounting policies are disclosed then it may be possible, when comparing one company with another, to make adjustments to the reported figures so as to put the accounts on a comparable basis.

A problem that arises in the use of published accounts is that the reporting entity may not be the business unit that the user is concerned with. For example, if a company is engaged in several types of activity then an employee in one particular section of the business will not be able to assess employment prospects in that particular part of the business by reference to the published accounts of the company as a whole. There will, of course, be a limited amount of segmental information published to comply with the Companies Act 1985.

These limitations do not mean that accounts are of no value. An awareness of the limitations will make the analyst more cautious in assessing accounting information, and this awareness is part of the skill needed in the interpretation of accounts.

Ratio analysis

A ratio is a way of expressing the relationship between two amounts as a proportion or percentage. This has the following advantages:

1. Many figures in the accounts are only meaningful when considered in relation to other figures. For example, if we wish to assess whether a profit of £50,000 is a 'good' result we would need to compare it with some measure of business size.
2. A computation of accounting ratios enables us to compare businesses of different size.
3. Some ratios enable us to gain a vision of the company's trading pattern, such as the 'number of days debtors' ratio discussed below.
4. Comparison with published industrial average ratios becomes possible.
5. Where information is supplied in confidence for the preparation of inter-firm comparative studies, the publication of data in ratio form makes it easier to preserve confidence.
6. The use of ratios can enable the analyst to relate accounting and non-accounting data. For example, several 'investor' ratios relate accounting data to the share price.
7. The preparation of a small number of key ratios simplifies the examination of the mass of data contained in the accounts.

It is, however, necessary to be cautious in the use of accounting ratios. We have already considered the limitations of accounting data, and it is important to bear in mind that these limitations also restrict the significance of ratios. It is important to remember that the computation of ratios is a tool to be used in interpretation, not an end in itself. There can sometimes be a danger, when computing accounting ratios, that the significance of individual amounts considered in isolation will not be observed. As we will see, there are a number of terms used in ratio analysis that can have several meanings, such as return on capital employed. It is necessary to be aware of these different possible meanings when using ratios, and to be careful when presenting ratios not to use ambiguous terminology. In short, when using ratio analysis the necessary skills cover not only the computation of accounting ratios, but also an understanding of their significance.

Sources of comparative data

Accounting data for a business can be compared with external or internal data. When making external comparisons there can be problems in deciding what type of business should be regarded as comparable; the problem is to find a business with a similar trading pattern, and the following factors might be considered:

1. **Type of industry.** This is the most common basis for making comparisons, since within each industry a similar trading pattern will be expected; however, it is necessary to remember that in industries

where there is a seasonal trading pattern balance sheets of businesses with different accounting dates may not be comparable. There may be problems in deciding how to define an industry; for example, a shipping company running passenger services might be classified as 'shipping', 'travel', or perhaps 'holiday'. There will also be problems of classification where a company engaged in several kinds of business activity is being considered.

2. **Nationality.** The legal and cultural framework within which a business operates can have a significant impact on the accounts, and normally comparison will be made with other companies operating in the same country. In the case of a large-scale business, such as motor manufacturing, there may not be enough businesses operating within the same national industry to make such comparisons, in which case comparison may be made with other businesses operating within similar environments, e.g. UK companies might be compared with competitors in other EEC countries. A multinational corporation may compare the accounts of divisions operating in different countries. Where a foreign country is particularly successful in a particular field, comparison might be made with the accounts of businesses in that country as a guide to the reasons for success.

3. **Regional area.** In some cases comparison between businesses in the same regional area may be appropriate. For example, we may find that hotels in London have a different trading pattern from hotels in seaside resorts.

4. **Size of business.** When using accounting ratios, the size of a company does not necessarily affect comparability. However, in certain types of business, size is likely to affect the trading pattern. For example, a chain of supermarkets has a different trading pattern to a small grocer's shop, even though both are in the 'food-retailing' industry.

The importance of making comparison with businesses having a similar trading pattern will depend on the ratio being considered. For example, almost every business employs assets with the objective of earning a return. Thus, in most cases ratios of return on capital will be comparable, with the exception of those businesses such as professional practices where the major asset of the business, goodwill, is normally not recorded at a meaningful amount in the balance sheet. By contrast, a ratio of stock turnover will depend on the nature of the industry.

Having defined the category of business with which comparison is to be made, it is possible to make comparison either with average ratios for that category or with other specific businesses. Data can be obtained:

1. In the case of limited companies, by obtaining copies of their accounts from the registrar of companies. In the case of a small company, the amount of data contained in the published accounts will be very limited.

2. By reference to published industrial average data. This can be obtained from government statistics and from the publications of a number of

private organizations, and these will be derived mainly from published accounts.

3. By subscribing to a scheme for the production of data for a particular type of business, participants being required to contribute to the costs of the scheme and to submit information about their own business. Such schemes are commonly run by professional and trade associations. They have the advantage of making available data that could not be derived from published accounts, which are then shared among participants on a basis that protects the anonymity of individual companies.

Internal sources of comparison are:

1. the accounts of the business for previous years. These are particularly useful for identifying trends;
2. the accounts of other divisions within a company or group of companies;
3. target ratios used inside the organization.

Conclusion

The interpretation of accounts involves an appreciation of the needs of individual users, an awareness of the limitations of published accounts for decision-making purposes, a thorough grasp of specific ratio-analysis techniques, and an understanding of the factors influencing comparison.

Note: In future chapters the use of specific techniques will be illustrated by reference to the example of Barchester plc presented in Appendix 1.

Notes

2   The assessment of the liquidity position

Introduction

All those concerned with an analysis of a set of accounts are likely to have an interest in assessing whether the business is going to be able to meet its liabilities as they fall due. The terms 'liquidity' and 'solvency' are used when talking about this aspect of a company's financial position. Some authorities make a distinction between 'liquidity', which is regarded as the short-term financial position, and 'solvency', which refers to long-term financial stability; other writers have regarded the two terms as inter-changeable. In this chapter we will consider some of the accounting ratios used to assess a company's financial stability in the short term.

Relating current assets to current liabilities

A normal starting point in any analysis of liquidity is to compare the total assets which are expected to turn into cash in the short term with total liabilities which have to be paid in the short term. Two ratios can be used for this.

1. The **current ratio**. This is computed as:

$$\frac{\text{Current assets}}{\text{Current liabilities}}$$

For our example Barchester plc this ratio might be computed:

$$\begin{array}{cc} 19X8 & 19X7 \\ \dfrac{1,400}{550} = 2.5 & \dfrac{1,215}{445} = 2.7 \end{array}$$

2. The **liquidity** ratio (also known as the **quick asset ratio** or the **acid test**). The objective of this ratio is to exclude from current assets those items which take a long time to turn into cash. The ratio is normally computed as:

$$\frac{\text{Current assets } - \text{ Stock}}{\text{Current liabilities}}$$

For our example Barchester plc this ratio might be computed:

$$\frac{19X8}{\frac{1,400-900}{550}} = 0.9 \qquad\qquad \frac{19X7}{\frac{1,215-696}{445}} = 1.2$$

This is the normal way of computing this ratio, and in the absence of any information to the contrary when this ratio is presented to us as, for example, an industrial average, we may assume that this has been the basis of computation. Sometimes the way in which the accounts are prepared provides an indication that items other than stock should be excluded; for example, where a prepayment is shown above the stock figure in the list of current assets then this would suggest that the item is less liquid than stock.

In a manufacturing business a fall in the liquidity ratio is likely to indicate imminent liquidity problems more rapidly than a fall in the current ratio. One possible source of liquidity problems arises when a company has suffered a drop in demand for its product; sales drop, with a consequent fall in debtors, while production continues resulting in a build-up of stock, so that the liquidity ratio falls but the current ratio actually increases. However, the liquidity ratio will only be relevant to companies that hold stock for any length of time or sell goods on credit. A retail store, for example, may well sell its goods for cash in a shorter time than the period of credit allowed by suppliers.

In practice both ratios are commonly used. Any difference between the pattern shown by the two will be attributable to differences in the stock-holding position.

When computing these ratios it is necessary to examine the accounts carefully to ensure that no current assets or current liabilities are classified under other headings, although such a situation should not arise in the case of a company complying with the requirements of the Companies Act 1985. One example would arise where a company with a debenture out-standing continues to classify this as a long-term loan in the balance sheet presented at the commencement of the year when the loan becomes repayable. Another issue that can arise is that an asset or liability that is in law receivable or payable within one year, and is therefore classified as current in the accounts, may in practice be a long-term item. A number of companies, for example, use a bank overdraft as a long-term source of finance, relying on the bank to renew the overdraft facility repeatedly even though the loan can be called in in the short-term.

Working capital activity ratios

When there is cause for concern as to the liquidity position of a company, the problem can be investigated further by looking at the relationship between individual items of working capital and the level of activity of the business. This approach cannot be applied to all current items, because some items, such as the taxation liability or the bank overdraft, are not directly linked with the level of activity. However, for stock, debtors and creditors, it is appropriate to look at the relationship with the level of activity. Each of the ratios we are going to look at can be computed either by reference to year end figures or by reference to the average of the opening and closing balances. For the purpose of illustration we will use the year end figures.

The stock figure is normally related to the level of activity by computing the **stock turnover ratio**. This term can mean two different things:

1. It can express the number of times that stock turns over during the year, and is computed as:

$$\frac{\text{Cost of sales}}{\text{Stock}}$$

For Barchester plc the ratio can be computed as:

$$\begin{array}{cc}
\textit{19X8} & \textit{19X7} \\
\dfrac{2,409}{900} = 2.7 & \dfrac{2,117}{696} = 3
\end{array}$$

This ratio has the merit of comparing 'like with like', because both stock and cost of sales are measured at cost. However, the cost of sales figure is not always shown in a set of company accounts.

2. It can express the relationship between stock and the sales for the year (otherwise referred to as 'turnover'). In this case the ratio will be computed as:

$$\frac{\text{Turnover}}{\text{Stock}}$$

On this basis, the ratio for Barchester plc will be:

$$\begin{array}{cc}
\textit{19X8} & \textit{19X7} \\
\dfrac{4,015}{900} = 4.5 & \dfrac{3,650}{696} = 5.2
\end{array}$$

Whichever method is used to compute a stock turnover ratio, the trend revealed is likely to be the same unless there is a material change in the gross profit percentage (considered in detail below). When making a comparison with an industrial average ratio, it is essential that the ratio for the company be computed in the same way as the industrial average has been computed. Under examination conditions, unless the question specifically states otherwise, stock turnover should be computed on the basis of the cost of sales figure where this is available. It is also possible to relate the stock figure to the cost of sales by calculating the number of days stock being:

$$\frac{\text{Stock}}{\text{Cost of sales}} \times 365$$

For Barchester plc this figure would be computed as:

$$
\begin{array}{cc}
\textit{19X8} & \textit{19X7} \\[4pt]
\dfrac{900}{2,409} \times 365 = 136 \text{ days} & \dfrac{696}{2,117} \times 365 = 120 \text{ days}
\end{array}
$$

This method of expressing the relationship between the stock figure and the cost of sales is useful because it enables the analyst to visualize the movement of stock. However, the figure is only meaningful where the level of activity does not fluctuate materially during the year, and where there are no special factors influencing the stock level.

Debtors can be related to the sales figure by computing the **number of days debtors**, computed as:

$$
\frac{\text{Debtors}}{\text{Sales}} \times 365
$$

For Barchester plc the amounts will be:

$$
\begin{array}{cc}
\textit{19X8} & \textit{19X7} \\[4pt]
\dfrac{480}{4,015} \times 365 = 44 \text{ days} & \dfrac{400}{3,650} \times 365 = 40 \text{ days}
\end{array}
$$

Note that only the **trade** debtors should be included in the computation of this ratio.

It would also be possible to compute a debtors turnover ratio similar to the stock turnover ratio. As with the number of days stock, this ratio is only meaningful where there is a constant level of sales throughout the year. The number of days debtors ratio is only representative of the number of days credit being taken by customers when all sales are on credit; where there is a mixture of cash and credit sales, a change in this ratio might represent a change in the mix of sales rather than any difference in the effectiveness of credit control. In principle, when calculating the number of days debtors we should exclude any element of Value Added Tax from the debtors figure, but in practice such an adjustment is not normally made; when making comparison between different companies in the same industry or between successive years of one company, the debtors figure in each set of accounts will normally be distorted in a similar way, so that the relative position will be the same whether an adjustment is made or not.

It is only possible to compute a number of days creditors ratio when a figure for purchases is available; in that case the ratio would be computed as:

$$
\frac{\text{Trade creditors}}{\text{Purchases}} \times 365
$$

The purchases figure is often not presented in the published accounts; sometimes it can be identified by reference to the total of bought-in costs shown in the value added statement. Where the purchases figure is not available, the relationship between trade creditors and the level of activity can be assessed by reference to the **creditors' turnover** figure, computed as:

$$\frac{\text{Sales}}{\text{Creditors}}$$

For Barchester plc this ratio will be:

19X8	*19X7*
$\dfrac{4,015}{260} = 15.4$	$\dfrac{3,650}{100} = 36.5$

As with the stock turnover ratio, the term 'creditors turnover' ratio could also refer to the number of times creditors turn over in the year computed as:

$$\frac{\text{Purchases}}{\text{Creditors}}$$

In practice, the ratio is unlikely to be computed in this form because when the purchases figure is available the number of days creditors will normally be computed.

An increased strain on liquidity can also arise because of an increase in sales leading to an increased working capital requirement. Therefore the **sales increase ratio** can be computed, being:

$$\frac{\text{Present year sales} - \text{Previous year sales}}{\text{Previous year sales}}$$

For our example this ratio is:

$$\frac{4,015 - 3,650}{3,650} = 10\%$$

Two possible problems can arise under examination conditions when computing the working capital activity ratios:

1. Sometimes examiners specify that the number of days in a year should be assumed to be some other figure than 365, either to simplify calculations or to express ratios in terms of working days. Activity ratios may also be expressed in terms of weeks rather than days.
2. It is not always clear, when examiners ask students to compute working capital activity ratios, whether these should be computed by reference to the year end balances or the average of opening and closing balances. Broadly speaking, if the examiner makes a point of giving the data that make it possible to use average figures then these should be used; conversely, if the data given are only sufficient to identify year end figures these should be used.

Conclusion

When assessing the liquidity position the analyst is concerned with the company's management of working capital. From the point of view of liquidity, increased current and liquidity ratios are a sign of a safer position, but conversely from the point of view of maximizing the return on funds employed in the business it is desirable to minimize the resources tied up in working capital. Good working capital management involves a compromise between the need for adequate liquidity and the achievement of a satisfactory return on capital. The desirable minimum ratios will vary according to the industry; for example, a retail store that turns over stock rapidly and makes cash sales can satisfactorily operate with a low current ratio, while a heavy engineering business with high levels of stock and work-in-progress, as well as sales made on credit, will show a far higher ratio.

Notes

3 Analysing the financial structure

Introduction

The way in which a business is financed can have a dramatic effect on success or failure. Ratio analysis can help us to understand the impact of financial structure on the business.

The nature of gearing

An analysis of the financial structure of a business is important both to the proprietors and to the creditors. Such an analysis is often relevant to an appraisal of the long-term financial stability of the business. Virtually any business will derive part of its resources from the proprietors and part from the creditors. Normally, the various creditors will receive a fixed consideration in exchange for the finance they have provided. In some cases, such as a debenture or a bank overdraft, this fixed consideration will take the form of an agreed rate of interest. In other cases, such as the trade creditors or the outstanding taxation liability, the liability will arise as a result of trading conventions and will not normally carry any interest charge. In either case the consideration paid by the company to the suppliers of borrowed funds will be a fixed amount, irrespective of the level of profits. Where a large part of the resources of the company are financed by borrowing and, as a result, there is a substantial fixed claim by the creditors on the company's earnings, then any fluctuation in the operating profit of the business will have a greater proportional effect on the residual profit belonging to the proprietors. This effect is generally described as 'gearing' in the UK and as 'leverage' in the USA. Sometimes the terms 'capital gearing' or 'financial leverage' are used. The effects of gearing can be illustrated by the following simple example:

Alpha Ltd and Beta Ltd are two companies in the same industry, each with total assets of £100,000. Each company is financed partly by the proprietors and partly by 15% debentures as follows:

| | Alpha | Beta |
	£	£
Proprietors' interest	80,000	40,000
15% debentures	20,000	60,000
	100,000	100,000
Total assets	100,000	100,000

Table 3.1 shows the effect of fluctuations in the operating profit upon the rate of return on the proprietors' iinterest, ignoring taxation. Column A shows that an operating profit of £15,000 results in both companies showing a rate of return on the proprietors' interest of 15%. Column B shows that if there is a 10% increase in this profit figure to £16,500 then the profit attributable to the proprietors rises by 12.5% for Alpha and by 25% for Beta, with similar effects on the rate of return on the proprietors' interests. Column C shows that a 10% drop in the operating profit compared to Column A produces a 12.5% drop in the profit attributable to the proprietors of Alpha and a 25% drop in the case of Beta. This effect can be measured by a ratio known as the **degree of capital gearing**, which is computed as:

$$\frac{\text{Profit before tax} + \text{Interest}}{\text{Profit before tax}}$$

For our example, taking a level of operating profit of £15,000, this ratio will be:

Table 3.1

Alpha

$$\frac{15,000}{12,000} = 1.25$$

Beta

$$\frac{15,000}{6,000} = 2.5$$

Thus:

$$\frac{\text{Fluctuation in}}{\text{operating profit}} \times \frac{\text{Degree of}}{\text{capital gearing}} = \frac{\text{Fluctuation in profit}}{\text{attributable to shareholders}}$$

From the point of view of creditors, the higher the level of gearing the higher the level of risk. In our example, the debenture holders of Alpha can expect to recover their loan unless more than 80% of the assets of the business are lost, whereas the debenture holders of Beta will not receive full repayment if more than 40% of the assets of the business are lost.

If a company can employ its resources in such a way as to earn a rate of return higher than the level of interest rates, then an increase in gearing will result in an increase in the profit attributable to shareholders; on the other hand, creditors will become less willing to lend to the company if gearing rises to a level where the risks are substantially increased. Thus an increase in gearing offers opportunities to boost the earnings of shareholders, but at the cost of increased risk and restrictions on the company's opportunities to make further borrowings.

Table 3.1

	Column A Profit of £15,000		Column B Profit of £16,500		Column C Profit of £13,500	
	Alpha £	Beta £	Alpha £	Beta £	Alpha £	Beta £
Operating profit	15,000	15,000	16,500	16,500	13,500	13,500
Interest	3,000	9,000	3,000	9,000	3,000	9,000
Profit attributable to shareholders	12,000	6,000	13,500	7,500	10,500	4,500
Return as a percentage of proprietors' interest	$\frac{12,000}{80,000}$ = 15%	$\frac{6,000}{40,000}$ = 15%	$\frac{13,500}{80,000}$ = 16.875%	$\frac{7,500}{40,000}$ = 18.75%	$\frac{10,500}{80,000}$ = 13.125%	$\frac{4,500}{40,000}$ = 11.25%

Preference shares are a source of finance that can be difficult to classify when trying to assess a company's financial structure. In law, preference shareholders are regarded as members of the company; in the event of a liquidation they receive no payment until the claims of all creditors have been satisfied in full, and preference dividends may only be paid out of profits. Thus from the point of view of creditors assessing the degree of risk involved in lending to the company, it would seem appropriate to classify preference shares as part of the proprietors' interest. On the other hand, preference shares carry the right to a fixed level of dividend, and do not share in the residual profits of the company. From the point of view of equity shareholders assessing the extent to which the company has been financed from other sources, it would seem appropriate to classify preference shares as a form of borrowing. In practice, it seems more common to regard preference shares as a form of borrowing.

There are two possible approaches to the measurement of gearing:

1. **Capital-based gearing ratios** express the relationship between the proprietors' interest and the other sources of finance.
2. **Income-based gearing ratios** express the relationship between the total income of the business and that part of the total income that has to be paid to creditors as finance charges.

Capital-based gearing ratios

If we consider the basic balance sheet equation: Proprietors' interest + Borrowings = Total assets, then we can see that there are a number of ways in which we can express the relationship between the proprietors' interest and the borrowings. Perhaps the simplest way of expressing the relationship is by the ratio:

Borrowings: Proprietors' interest

In the USA this is commonly referred to as the **debt: equity ratio**, in which case 'debt' normally means total borrowings.

The relationship can also be expressed as a proportion or percentage as:

$$\frac{\text{Borrowings}}{\text{Proprietors' interest} + \text{Borrowings}}$$

The advantages of expressing the relationship in this way are:

1. The calculation will always produce a proportion less than one, unless there is a negative proprietors' interest.
2. An increase in this ratio indicates increased gearing, and vice versa.
3. As we will see below, a ratio computed in this way can be used to explain the differences between return on capital employed ratios computed on different bases.

'Borrowings' can mean either total or long-term borrowings.

For Barchester plc we can calculate this ratio in two ways:

1. Based on long-term borrowings:

$$\begin{array}{cc} \textit{19X8} & \textit{19X7} \\[4pt] \dfrac{1{,}000}{1{,}000 + 1{,}850} = 35\% & \dfrac{1{,}000}{1{,}000 + 1{,}750} = 36\% \end{array}$$

2. Based on total borrowings:

$$\begin{array}{cc} \dfrac{550 + 1{,}000}{550 + 1{,}000 + 1{,}850} = 46\% & \dfrac{445 + 1{,}000}{445 + 1{,}000 + 1{,}750} = 45\% \end{array}$$

In practice, it may well be useful to compute gearing ratios related both to long-term and total borrowings. On the one hand, where current liabilities are included in borrowings the gearing ratio may be subject to fluctuation, or even deliberate manipulation, through exceptional circumstances at the year end. On the other hand, a company may have a policy of financing part of its resources on a permanent basis by recurring short-term borrowing. Thus, to ensure a complete picture, it is advisable to compute and consider ratios computed on both bases.

It is also possible to compute a 'proprietorship' ratio, being:

$$\frac{\text{Proprietor's interest}}{\text{Proprietor's interest} + \text{Borrowings}}$$

which expresses the same relationship.

Income-based gearing ratios

Income-based gearing ratios express the relationship between operating profit and interest charges. The most common method for expressing this relationship is the **interest cover ratio**, sometimes referred to as 'times interest earned', computed as:

$$\frac{\text{Profit before tax} + \text{Interest charges}}{\text{Interest charges}}$$

This ratio is normally computed by reference to total interest charges. In the case of Barchester plc the ratio will be:

$$\begin{array}{cc} \textit{19X8} & \textit{19X7} \\[4pt] \dfrac{503}{100} = 5 & \dfrac{633}{100} = 6.3 \end{array}$$

The ratio tells us the number of times interest is covered by profit in the year.

It is also possible to compute a ratio of long-term interest cover, but this is not common in practice.

We have already considered the 'degree of capital gearing' ratio. In countries such as the UK, where a 'partial deferral' approach to deferred tax is in force, this ratio cannot be used to explain after-tax profit, but it can be used to explain the effect of a fluctuation in operating profit on the pre-tax profit available to shareholders.

The ratio will be computed as:

$$\frac{\text{Profit before tax} + \text{Interest charges}}{\text{Profit before tax}}$$

For Barchester plc the ratio will be computed:

19X8	19X7
$\frac{503}{403} = 1.25$	$\frac{633}{533} = 1.18$

Interpreting the gearing ratios

We have seen that there are a number of ways of computing ratios that measure gearing. For example, Table 3.2 summarizes four different ratios we have managed to compute for Barchester plc. Each of these ratios may be appropriate for different purposes. We can illustrate this by considering the various needs of shareholders and creditors in analysing the accounts, and linking these to the ratios for Barchester plc.

Ordinary shareholders will be interested in:

1.   Estimating the extent to which any change in operating profit will be magnified in its impact on profit available to shareholders as a result of gearing. Ratio 4 (see Table 3.2) reflects the impact of gearing on profit available to shareholders. The effect relates to pre-tax profit and there is no formula available that can estimate the effect on profit after tax. In the case of Barchester plc the ratio indicates that the effects of gearing on fluctuations in profit available to shareholders are increasing.
2.   Assessing the company's ability to make interest payments. Ratio 3, total interest cover, indicates that the company is becoming more vulnerable in this respect but the ratio, at 5, indicates that there is still a substantial margin of cover.
3.   Judging the overall level of risk arising from the company's gearing position. Ratio 1, measuring total borrowings in relation to total resources, will be of particular interest.
4.   Assessing what the directors' policy on gearing is. For this purpose the position relating to long-term funds is likely to be a better indicator,

Table 3.2   Gearing Ratios for Barchester plc

	19X8	19X7
1. Capital-based ratio (based on total borrowings)	46%	45%
2. Capital-based ratio (based on long-term borrowings)	35%	36%
3. Total interest cover	5	6.3
4. Degree of capital gearing	1.25	1.18

since this is not subject to short-term fluctuations. Ratio 2 is likely to be computed for this purpose.

Creditors are likely to be interested in:

1. The company's ability to meet interest payments. Ratio 3, interest cover, is likely to be the best indicator.
2. The company's ability to repay loans on the due date. For this purpose a cash-flow forecast would be the ideal tool, and failing this an analysis of the accounts might concentrate on looking at profitability trends and likely asset replacement requirements. The gearing ratios indicate how reliant the company is on borrowed funds, and from this point of view Ratio 1 seems particularly relevant.
3. The amount they are likely to realize in the event of a liquidation. Since the accounts do not normally include information on the net realizable value of assets, ratio analysis techniques cannot be applied directly to this issue. An examination of any data in the accounts on security for loans would be of interest.

'Off balance sheet' finance

It is possible for a company to find part of its requirements for finance by contriving to enjoy the use of assets that it does not own itself by means of a legal agreement that gives the company all the benefits, risks and obligations of ownership. One example of such an arrangement arises where a company enters into an agreement to lease items that would otherwise be purchased as fixed assets. When a long-term agreement to lease such items is made, the commercial substance is similar to the position where a fixed asset is purchased, financed by a secured loan, the lease payments being similar to repayment of principal and interest by instalments.

In the UK SSAP 21 now requires companies to account for such 'finance leases' in accordance with their commercial substance rather than their

Table 3.3

| | Turnover at £100,000 | | | | Turnover increases by 10% | | | |
| | Delta Ltd | | Gamma Ltd | | Delta Ltd | | Gamma Ltd | |
	£000	£000	£000	£000	£000	£000	£000	£000
Sales		100		100		110		110
Expenses								
Fixed	50		20		50		20	
Variable	50		60		33		66	
		80		80		83		86
Profit		20		20		27		24
% increase in profit						35%		20%

legal form, by recording the leased assets and the lease commitments in the balance sheet. However, in practice companies are able to avoid this requirement by entering into carefully contrived lease arrangements which just fall outside the technical definition of a finance lease. Thus, in assessing the true gearing position analysts must scrutinize lease commitments carefully.

The link with operational gearing

In the UK the term 'gearing' has traditionally been used to describe the effects of the financial structure of the company. However, recently some writers have followed US practice in distinguishing between **capital gearing**, being the effects of the financial structure, and **operational gearing**, being the effects of the operating structure.

To illustrate the effects of operational leverage let us consider two companies:

1. Delta Ltd has fixed costs of £50,000 per year and variable costs of 30% of sales.
2. Gamma Ltd has fixed costs of £20,000 per year and variable costs of 60% of sales.

Table 3.3 illustrates that on the basis of these figures both companies make the same profit at a sales level of £100,000 but that if sales increase by 10% the profit of Delta increases by 35%, that of Gamma by 20%. It is possible to identify a ratio, the 'degree of operational gearing', that identifies the impact on operating profit of any percentage movement in turnover. This ratio is computed as:

$$\frac{\text{Sales less variable costs}}{\text{Sales less (variable + fixed costs)}}$$

For our example this ratio, at a sales level of £10,000, will be:

$$\begin{array}{cc} \textit{Delta} & \textit{Gamma} \\ \dfrac{100 - 30}{100 - (30 + 50)} = 3.5 & \dfrac{100 - 60}{100 - (60 + 20)} = 2 \end{array}$$

With this ratio we can estimate the effect of any fluctuation in turnover on profit attributable to shareholders. One suspects that traditionally the link between capital gearing and operational gearing has not been drawn in the UK because one is normally considered by the financial accountant and the other by the management accountant. However, it is possible to envisage situations where a management decision could have an impact on both types of gearing, and it would be desirable to consider the two together. For example, if a company is considering the purchase of a machine with borrowed funds to perform a function previously carried out by subcontractors, there is a potential impact both on capital gearing, because of the new borrowing, and on operational gearing, because of the fixed costs of running the machine; the two aspects combined may involve a substantial increase in risk.

Conclusion

An analysis of a company's financial structure involves looking at both the balance sheet and the profit and loss account. If we are to understand the full 'gearing' effect we must also look at the balance between fixed and variable costs.

Notes

4 Analysis of performance

Introduction

This is the most difficult area of ratio analysis. When looking at the company's liquidity position we were faced with the simple issue of whether or not the working capital would be adequate to enable the company to continue trading, while the analysis of financial structure dealt with a broader range of questions each of which in itself was fairly easily defined. An assessment of what constitutes adequate performance, on the other hand, involves a broader range of judgements as to what is being aimed at. In assessing performance we will need to rely on profit and loss figures; these are particularly dependent on management's judgement and choice of accounting policies. Finally, the published accounts are unlikely to contain the full range of detail we might desire. Thus we will find when assessing performance that, because of the greater complexity of our objectives, we will have to consider a greater range of ratios and at the same time the conclusions we reach are likely to be more tentative than when assessing other aspects of a company's position.

The primary ratio

The ratio of **return on capital employed (ROCE)**, often described as the primary ratio, is the normal starting point when assessing a company's performance. This ratio relates the income earned from the company's activities to the resources employed by the company. The ratio is compared as:

$$\frac{\text{Return}}{\text{Capital}}$$

Normally 'return' is taken as profit before extraordinary items, since by definition these items fall outside the scope of the company's normal operations. This does not mean that extraordinary items should be ignored by the analyst, but that their significance should be assessed as a separate exercise from the examination of the company's performance.

There are a number of different ways of computing ratios of return on capital employed. The following are the most common:

1. **After-tax return on equity.** This would be computed as:

$$\frac{\text{Profit after tax} - \text{Preference dividend}}{\text{Ordinary share capital} + \text{Reserves}}$$

For Barchester plc the ratio would be computed as:

19X8	*19X7*
$\frac{260}{1,850} = 14.1\%$	$\frac{347}{1,750} = 19.8\%$

2. **Pre-tax return on equity.** This would be computed as:

$$\frac{\text{Profit before tax} - \text{Preference dividend}}{\text{Ordinary share capital} + \text{Reserves}}$$

For Barchester plc the ratio would be computed as:

19X8	*19X7*
$\frac{403}{1,850} = 21.8\%$	$\frac{533}{1,750} = 30.5\%$

3. **Pre-tax return on long-term funds employed.** This would be computed as:

$$\frac{\text{Profit before tax} + \text{Long-term interest}}{\text{Share capital} + \text{Reserves} + \text{Long-term loans}}$$

The definition of 'return' in this case includes the preference dividend and interest because the definition of 'capital' includes preference shares and long-term loans. One problem that can arise in practice when trying to compute this ratio is that the accounts do not always identify the amount of long-term interest separately.

For Barchester plc the long-term interest on £1,000,000 of 10% debentures is £100,000, so that the whole of the interest charge shown in the profit and loss account relates to this long-term loan. Therefore the ratio will be:

19X8	*19X7*
$\frac{503}{1,000 + 1,850} = 17.6\%$	$\frac{633}{1,000 + 1,750} = 23\%$

4. **Pre-tax return on total funds employed.** This would be computed as:

$$\frac{\text{Profit before tax} + \text{Total interest}}{\text{Share capital} + \text{Reserves} + \text{Total liabilities}}$$

For Barchester plc the ratio would therefore be computed:

19X8	*19X7*
$\frac{503}{1,850 + 1,000 + 550} = 14.8\%$	$\frac{633}{1,750 + 1,000 + 445} = 19.8\%$

The two major areas of difference between the various ratios we have computed relate to:

1. The definition of 'capital' we have used. Each definition of 'capital' implies its own definition of 'return'.
2. The question as to whether pre-tax or post-tax profit should be considered.

The most useful definition of capital depends upon the purpose for which the ratio is computed. For shareholders, or for those trying to assess how shareholders are likely to react to the accounts, the return on equity figures are likely to be particularly important. On the other hand, if we are trying to assess how effectively management have employed the resources committed to the business then a definition of capital that takes into account borrowed funds will be more useful; in that case a definition of capital as 'total funds' gives a fuller view of the position, but where short-term borrowings are subject to erratic fluctuations a definition of capital as 'long-term funds' may be more useful.

The arguments in favour of using after-tax profit are:

1. Taxation has to be paid as a result of the activities of the business and, although by convention shown as an appropriation of profit, is no different in substance to any other business expense.
2. One of management's functions is to obtain sound advice on tax planning, and an analysis of the company's performance should take into account the question of how effectively this has been done.
3. The published earnings per share figure is based on profit after tax, and a ratio computed on the basis of after-tax profit is more relevant to explaining fluctuations in this figure.

On the other hand, it can be argued in favour of taking profit before tax that:

1. SSAP 15 on deferred taxation, prescribing a partial deferral approach, involves a considerable degree of estimation and judgement in assessing the year's tax charge, so that the tax charge in the accounts of different companies may not be comparable.
2. Where the taxation rate changes from one year to another the comparison of ratios will be distorted.
3. The company's taxation position is best judged separately from other aspects of company performance.

In practice, a full ratio analysis exercise is likely to involve the computation of several ROCE ratios. A three-stage process may well give the clearest picture:

1. Compute the after-tax return on equity. This gives us an overall picture of what has been achieved on behalf of ordinary shareholders during the year.
2. Compute the pre-tax return on equity. This gives us a picture of what has been achieved on behalf of ordinary shareholders ignoring the effects of taxation. If this ratio gives a substantially different picture to

the after-tax return on equity then we would investigate the tax position further, possibly by computing the ratio:

$$\frac{\text{Tax charge}}{\text{Pre-tax profit}}$$

as a starting point.

3. As a measure of the operating performance, compute either return on long-term funds or return on total funds, choosing between the two ratios on the basis of the criteria laid out above in our discussion of gearing (see pages 16–21). Any difference between this ratio and the pre-tax return on equity will be explained by changes in gearing, which we can investigate further by looking at the gearing ratios previously computed, and also at the ratio:

$$\frac{\text{Interest charges}}{\text{Borrowed funds}}$$

There are a number of adjustments that, in some circumstances, might be made to the ratio of return on total assets in order to give a clearer view of how effectively management have employed the resources of the business:

1. The income from investments and associated companies may be excluded from 'return', and the related assets deducted from 'capital'.
2. Where a company owning its own premises is compared with a company renting premises, then the first company might be regarded as carrying on a property investment activity in combination with its trading activities. In that case the ratios can be made comparable either:
    (a) by deducting a notional rent figure from 'return' and the net book value of the property from 'capital' in the case of the first company;
    or
    (b) by adding back the rent to the 'return' and adding the value of the property to 'capital', in the case of the second company.
3. Where two companies being compared use different accounting policies, adjustments might be made to reflect common accounting policies for both companies.

The secondary ratios

Any ratio of return on capital employed can be analysed into the secondary ratios, being the **net profit percentage** and the **asset turnover ratio**, since:

$$\frac{\text{Return}}{\text{Turnover}} \times \frac{\text{Turnover}}{\text{Capital}} = \frac{\text{Return}}{\text{Capital}}$$

The net profit percentage relates the performance achieved by the company to the level of activity, while the asset turnover ratio expresses the relationship between the level of activity and the resources employed by the business.

Although any ROCE ratio can, in principle, be analysed into the secondary ratios, in practice the objective of calculating these ratios is to analyse management's achievements in running the business. Therefore the ratios are normally computed in relation to either the return on long-term funds employed or the return on total funds employed, depending on which is regarded as the most meaningful performance figure. For our example, Barchester plc, we can compute secondary ratios relating to return on total assets as follows:

1. **Net profit percentage:**

$$
\begin{array}{cc}
19X8 & 19X7 \\
\dfrac{503}{4,015} = 12.5\% & \dfrac{633}{3,650} = 17.3\%
\end{array}
$$

2. **Asset turnover:**

$$
\begin{array}{cc}
19X8 & 19X7 \\
\dfrac{4,015}{1,850 + 1,000 + 550} = 1.18 & \dfrac{3,650}{1,750 + 1,000 + 445} = 1.14
\end{array}
$$

We can verify these figures by checking that they multiply back to the return on total funds as computed above:

$$
\begin{array}{l}
19X8: \quad 12.5\% \times 1.18 = 14.8\% \\
19X7: \quad 17.3\% \times 1.14 = 19.8\%
\end{array}
$$

We can now see that the asset turnover ratio is virtually unchanged, while the net profit percentage has fallen significantly. In this particular case, therefore, we would further investigate the net profit position.

Since all business operations have the objective of earning profit with the resources they employ, we would expect the return on capital employed ratio to be comparable across a number of industries. However, the relationship between the secondary ratios will vary enormously between different industries. For example, a chain of retail food shops selling its stock very rapidly for cash would have a high asset turnover, but a low net profit percentage, compared to most other industries.

INVESTIGATING THE NET PROFIT PERCENTAGE

Any investigation of the net profit percentage is restricted by the amount of detail given in the profit and loss account. Where the information is available, it is normal to compute the gross profit percentage, being:

$$
\frac{\text{Gross profit}}{\text{Sales}}
$$

For Barchester plc this will be:

$$
\begin{array}{cc}
19X8 & 19X7 \\
\dfrac{1,606}{4,015} = 40\% & \dfrac{1,533}{3,650} = 42\%
\end{array}
$$

A change in the gross profit percentage can be attributable to a wide range of causes, including:

1. A change in the sales mix. Where a business sells a variety of goods, sold at different mark-ups on cost, a change in the mix of goods sold will result in a change in the gross profit percentage.
2. A change in the cost of goods purchased. Such a change may arise because of overall market conditions. It may also arise because of a change in the purchasing pattern of the business itself; for example, if the trade of the business expands it may be possible to obtain discounts for larger purchases of goods. When the cost of goods purchased changes it may be that management will choose to maintain the level of gross profit in monetary rather than percentage terms. Let us imagine a business that buys widgets for £30 each and sells them for £50 each. Let us suppose the purchase price doubles to £60 while the gross profit per widget remains at £20, giving a selling price of £80, then:

	Old price £	*New price* £
Selling price	50	80
Cost	30	60
Gross profit	20	20
Gross profit %	$\dfrac{20}{50} = 40\%$	$\dfrac{20}{50} = 25\%$

3. A change in the selling price. Such a change may arise because of market conditions. It may also arise because of management policy. For example, management may decide to cut prices in order to attract new custom and so increase turnover; where such a policy is successful, we would expect to find a fall in the gross profit percentage compensated for by an increase in asset turnover.
4. Accounting error. The gross profit percentage will be particularly distorted where there is an error in the stock figure, since such an error will have an equal and opposite effect in the following accounting period.
5. Clearance of slow moving stock. When old stock is cleared by special low selling prices, the gross profit percentage will be distorted in that accounting period.
6. Removal of stock other than by sale. Where stock is lost through such causes as deterioration, pilfering or flood damage, then unless these causes can be identified and accounted for separately the gross profit percentage will be distorted.

There are two ways in which we can examine expenses:

1. We can express expenses as a percentage of turnover. For Barchester plc these ratios are:

(a)   *Distribution costs:*

19X8	*19X7*
$\dfrac{803}{4,015} = 20\%$	$\dfrac{660}{3,650} = 18.1\%$

(b)   *Administration costs:*

19X8	*19X7*
$\dfrac{300}{4,015} = 7.5\%$	$\dfrac{240}{3,650} = 6.6\%$

2.   When comparing successive years for one company, the increase or decrease in each category of expense can be expressed as a percentage. Thus for Barchester plc the increases during 19X8 are:

(a)   *Distribution costs:* $\dfrac{803 - 660}{660} = 22\%$

(b)   *Administration costs:* $\dfrac{300 - 240}{240} = 25\%$

Ideally, variable costs would be related to turnover, while fixed costs would be compared directly with the previous year; in practice, it is not normally possible to analyse costs in this way on the basis of the published accounts.

INVESTIGATING ASSET TURNOVER

The asset turnover ratio can be investigated further by relating each type of asset to turnover. Thus for Barchester plc we might compute fixed asset turnover as:

19X8	*19X7*
$\dfrac{4,015}{2,000} = 2$	$\dfrac{3,650}{1,980} = 1.8$

The relationship between the various current assets and the level of activity can be expressed in the same way, but is more likely to be expressed in the ways we have already considered in discussing the various working capital activity ratios.

Even where total asset turnover does not change, there may be a change in the way in which the business is managed so that some individual asset turnover ratios increase while others decrease. This is the case for Barchester plc, where an increased level of activity in relation to plant roughly compensates for relaxed working capital control.

Market share

An interesting ratio, which cannot be derived directly from the accounts, is the percentage of the market for its product that the company holds. As we have seen, analysis both of the expenses and of assets links to turnover. The market share ratio relates the company's turnover to the industrial environment.

Conclusion

The after-tax return on equity shows what has been achieved on behalf of shareholders. By going back to the return on long-term or total funds we can isolate the impact of tax and gearing. With the secondary ratios we can then examine how management have run the business.

Notes

5   Investor ratios

Introduction

A number of ratios relate the accounts to individual shareholders.

Earnings per share

The most complex investor ratio is the earnings per share ratio; this is the one ratio that is the subject of an accounting standard, SSAP 3. The basic principle is that the ratio is computed as:

$$\frac{\text{Earnings}}{\text{Number of ordinary shares}}$$

Three problems arise in computing this ratio:

1. How to define 'earnings'.
2. How to compute the number of shares. SSAP 3 defines this as the number of ordinary shares in issue and ranking for dividend during the year, but problems of definition arise where there is a new issue of shares during a year.
3. How to report the potential effects of any existing commitment to issue new shares; these effects are referred to as 'dilution'.

SSAP 3 puts forward solutions to each of these problems, which we will consider in detail below. To illustrate the application of SSAP 3 we will refer to the example 'Esmond plc' laid out in Table 5.1.

Examples of share capital position
Each of these examples is independent of the others:

1. Throughout 19X2 and 19X3 there were 8,000,000 ordinary shares of 25p in issue and ranking for dividend.
2. At 1 January 19X2 there were 8,000,000 ordinary shares of 25p in issue — on 1 July 19X3 a further 1,000,000 ordinary shares were issued at full market price.
3. At 1 January 19X2 there were 8,000,000 ordinary shares of 25p in issue.

Table 5.1   Esmond plc — profit and loss account extracts for the year to 31 December 19X3

	19X3 £000	19X3 £000	19X2 £000	19X2 £000
Profit before taxation		2,000		1,800
Taxation:				
Corporation tax	700		600	
Irrecoverable ACT	200		—	
		900		600
Profit after taxation		1,100		1,200
Extraordinary items		150		—
Profit after taxation and extraordinary items		950		1,200
Dividends:				
Preference	100		100	
Ordinary	500		500	
		600		600
Retained profit		350		600

On 1 July 19X3 a bonus issue of 1,000,000 ordinary shares was made.

4.   At 1 January 19X2 there were 8,000,000 ordinary shares of 25p in issue. On 1 July 19X3 1,000,000 new shares were issued in a rights issue at a price of £1.60. The market price immediately prior to the issue was £2.50.

5.   Throughout 19X2 and 19X3 there were 8,000,000 ordinary shares of 25p in issue and ranking for dividend. In addition 1,000,000 ordinary shares of 25p had been issued on 1 January 19X3 at full market price and these will rank for dividend as from 1 January 19X5.

6.   Throughout 19X2 and 19X3 there were 8,000,000 ordinary shares of 25p in issue and ranking for dividend. In addition, on 1 January 19X2 there was issued £2,000,000 of 11% convertible loan stock, convertible at a price of £2 per share on or after 1 January 19X5.

7.   Throughout 19X2 and 19X3 there was 8,000,000 ordinary shares of 25p in issue. On 1 January 19X2 there were granted options to buy 1,000,000 shares at a price of £2.30 per share on any date during 19X6. On both 31 December 19X1 and 31 December 19X2 the closing price of 2½% consolidated stock was £25. For all examples assume a corporation tax rate of 50%.

DEFINITION OF EARNINGS

SSAP 3 defines earnings as profit after tax, minority interest and preference dividends and before extraordinary items. Thus for Esmond plc, on the basis of the share capital position laid out in example 1 above, earnings per share will be computed as:

$$\frac{19X3}{1,100-100} = 12.5p \qquad \frac{19X2}{1,200-100} = 13.7p$$

$$\frac{1,100-100}{8,000} = 12.5p \qquad \frac{1,200-100}{8,000} = 13.7p$$

This is known as the 'net' basis. There is a view that where part of the tax charge consists of irrecoverable advance corporation tax (ACT) this amount should not be taken into account in computing the earnings per share, because irrecoverable ACT arises as a result of the company's dividend policy and is therefore not comparable from year to year or between companies. Earnings per share may therefore be computed on the 'nil' basis, excluding irrecoverable ACT from the computation. For Esmond plc the 19X3 earnings per share on the nil basis, on the basis of the share capital position in example 1, would be:

$$\frac{1,100+200-100}{8,000} = 15p$$

SSAP 3 requires listed companies to show the earnings per share on the net basis, and strongly recommends that material earnings per share on the nil basis should also be shown.

NUMBER OF SHARES

SSAP 3 identifies three situations where there may be a change in the share capital during the year:

1. **An issue of shares at full market price.** In this case the new resources introduced will increase the earning power of the business, while the increased earnings must be spread over a greater number of shares. The number of shares will therefore be computed on the average basis, weighted by reference to time. Thus in the case of Esmond plc on the basis of example 2. The average ordinary shares in issue for 19X3 will be:

$$
\begin{array}{ll}
6/12 \times 8,000,000 & 4,000,000 \\
6/12 \times 9,000,000 & 4,500,000 \\
\hline
& 8,500,000
\end{array}
$$

So that earnings per share on the net basis will be computed as:

$$\frac{19X3}{1,100-100} = 11.8p \qquad \frac{19X2}{1,200-100} = 13.7p$$

$$\frac{1,100-100}{8,500} = 11.8p \qquad \frac{1,200-100}{8,000} = 13.7p$$

2. **A bonus issue of shares.** This has no effect on the earning power of the business, because no new resources are introduced. The only effect is to increase the number of shares in issue over which earnings must be spread. Accordingly, SSAP 3 proposes that earnings per share be computed by reference to the number of ordinary shares in issue following the bonus issue, and the corresponding amount for the

previous year should be adjusted to reflect the bonus issue. At the end of 19X3 we would therefore disclose earnings per share for Esmond plc, on the assumption laid down in example 2, on the net basis, as:

$$\frac{1,100 - 100}{9,000} \qquad \frac{1,200 - 100}{9,000} = 12.2p$$

3. **A rights issue.** In this case the issue combines the characteristics of a bonus issue and an issue at full price. In order to estimate the relative importance of these two elements, SSAP 3 recommends computation of the 'theoretical ex-rights price', computed by reference to the terms of the rights issue as:

$$\left(\begin{array}{c}\text{Number of shares}\\ \text{prior to issue} \times \text{Market}\\ \text{price prior to issue}\end{array}\right) + \left(\begin{array}{c}\text{Number of shares}\\ \text{issued} \times \text{Issue}\\ \text{price}\end{array}\right) = \left(\begin{array}{c}\text{Theoretical}\\ \text{ex-rights}\\ \text{price}\end{array}\right)$$

For Esmond plc this price, based on example 4, is:

$$\begin{array}{rl}8 \times 2.50 =& 20.00\\ 1 \times 1.60 =& \underline{1.60}\\ \overline{9}\text{ shares} =& \overline{21.60}\end{array}$$

Therefore 1 share $= \dfrac{21.6}{9} = \underline{2.40}$

A weighted average number of shares is then computed, multiplying the number of shares in issue prior to the rights issue by the factor:

$$\frac{\text{Actual cum rights price}}{\text{Theoretical ex-rights price}}$$

Pursuing example 4 for Esmond plc the number of ordinary shares in issue for 19X3 will be:

$$\begin{array}{l}6/12 \times 8,000 \times \dfrac{2.50}{2.40} = 4,167\\[2mm] 6/12 \times 9,000 \qquad\quad\ = \underline{4,500}\\[1mm] \qquad\qquad\qquad\qquad\quad \overline{8,667}\end{array}$$

The corresponding earnings per share figure for the previous year is adjusted, in order to reflect the bonus element in the issue, by the factor:

$$\frac{\text{Theoretical ex-rights price}}{\text{Actual cum rights price}}$$

Thus we would compute the earnings of Esmond plc on the net basis as:

$$\begin{array}{cc}19X3 & 19X2\\ \dfrac{1,100 - 100}{8,667} = 11.5p & \qquad 13.7p \times \dfrac{2.40}{2.50} = 13.2p\end{array}$$

DILUTION

The third problem arising when computing earnings per share is dilution. SSAP 3 requires companies to disclose a figure for diluted earnings per share where the possible dilution exceeds 5% of the basic earnings per share figure. The three main types of potential dilution are:

1. Where shares already in issue do not yet rank for dividend. The diluted earnings per share are computed on the basis of total ordinary shares in issue. Thus for Esmond plc, on the basis of example 5, we would compute the diluted earnings per share for 19X3 on the net basis as:

$$\frac{1,100 - 100}{9,000} - 11.1p$$

2. Where the prospective dilution arises because there are in issue convertible preference shares or loan stock. In this case it is necessary to adjust the earnings figure by the amount of loan interest, net of tax relief, or preference dividend, which would cease to be paid on conversion, as well as adjusting the number of shares. If we take example 6 for Esmond plc, the saving on interest in the event of conversion would be:

	£
£2,000,000 at 11%	220,000
Less tax at 50 %	110,000
	110,000

so that the diluted earnings per share on the net basis will be:

$$\frac{1,100 - 100 + 110}{9,000} = 12.3p \qquad \frac{1,200 - 100 + 110}{9,000} = 13.4p$$

$$19X3 \qquad\qquad\qquad\qquad 19X2$$

The corresponding amount for the earnings per share figure should only be adjusted to the extent that the prospective dilution may still occur.

3. Where options exist to acquire shares it is necessary to estimate the income that would be generated if the options were exercised and the funds recived were employed in the company's business. For this purpose SSAP 3 suggests that the income to be generated should be assumed to be equal to the amount that would have been earned by investing the whole of the proceeds of the share issue in 2½% consolidated stock at the closing price ruling on the date immediately prior to the commencement of the accounting period. For Esmond plc these earnings, on the assumptions made in example 7, would both in 19X2 and 19X3 be:

	£
2.30 × 1,000,000 × 2.5/2.5 − 230,000	
Less tax at 50%	115,000
	115,000

On the net basis earnings per share will be:

$$\frac{19X3}{1,100 - 100 + 115} = 12.4\text{p} \qquad \frac{19X2}{1,200 - 100 + 115} = 13.5\text{p}$$
$$\frac{1,100 - 100 + 115}{9,000} = 12.4\text{p} \qquad \frac{1,200 - 100 + 115}{9,000} = 13.5\text{p}$$

Other related ratios

The main value of the earnings per share ratio is that it enables the individual shareholder to relate the figures in the profit and loss account to their own shareholding. In the case of a listed company it is possible to use this ratio as the basis for computing the **price earnings ratio**, often abbreviated to P/E ratio, computed as:

$$\frac{\text{Share price}}{\text{Earnings per share}}$$

This ratio varies with the share price. Let us suppose that we wish to compute this ratio for Esmond plc on a date when the share price is £2.45 and the 19X3 accounts have already been published then, taking the figures from example 1 on the net basis, the ratio will be:

$$\frac{2.45}{0.125} = 19.6$$

The ratio can be computed in relation to earnings per share calculated on any basis.

The P/E ratio enables the analyst to estimate the confidence that the stock market has in the company. A low P/E ratio suggests a lack of confidence in the company's ability to maintain earnings, while a high P/E ratio suggests a belief that the company is expected to increase earnings in the future.

Another ratio that links in with the share price is the **dividend yield ratio**, computed as:

$$\frac{\text{Dividend per ordinary share}}{\text{Share price}}$$

In the case of Esmond plc the dividend per ordinary share, based on example 1, is:

$$\frac{500}{8,000} = 6.25$$

so that if the share price is £2.45, dividend yield will be:

$$\frac{6.25}{2.45} = 2.6\%$$

The dividend yield shows the return currently earned in the form of dividends from an investment in the shares; future returns will be affected by changes in the rate of dividend and movements in the share price.

The **dividend cover ratio** shows the number of times the dividend is covered by earnings, and is computed as:

$$\frac{\text{Earnings per share}}{\text{Dividend per share}}$$

In the case of Esmond plc the 19X3 ratio, based on example 1 and the net basis, will be:

$$\frac{12.5}{6.25} = 2$$

Conclusion

The earnings per share ratio, reported daily in the financial press as the P/E ratio, is the most widely quoted piece of data from a company's accounts.

Notes

6 Other tools of interpretation

Introduction

In this chapter we consider a number of other interpretation tools: trend statements, common size statements and multivariate analysis.

Trend statements

Trend statements are more commonly prepared for profit and loss information, by choosing one year as the base year and expressing similar items of other years as a percentage of that base year. For example, for Barchester plc we might prepare a simple trend statement to compare 19X8 with 19X7 as follows:

	19X7	19X8
Turnover	100	110
Cost of sales	100	114
Distribution costs	100	122
Administrative expenses	100	125
Taxation	100	77

Normally, a trend statment would cover a period of at least five years. This is convenient way of presenting data for a large number of years, and can be helpful in highlighting trends. However, when presented with data in this form it is sometimes useful if we recompute each individual year's movement as compared with the previous year. For example, suppose we are presented with the following trend data for the sales of two companies, Eames Ltd and Crosby Ltd, over a five-year period:

	19X2	19X3	19X4	19X5	19X6
Eames	100	110	130	160	200
Crosby	100	150	210	240	250

If we restate these data in terms of the increase in sales achieved by each company we would show:

	19X3	19X4	19X5	19X6
Eames	10%	18%	23%	25%
Crosby	50%	40%	14%	4%

The trend statement indicated that in each year it would be correct to state that Crosby had expanded sales more rapidly than Eames since 1982. On the other hand, the data on increase in sales each year indicate that the rate of increase in sales is on the rise for Eames and on the decline for Crosby, with the former company now increasing sales at a very much faster rate. Thus both types of analysis can give us a useful insight.

Common size statements

A common size statement expresses the amounts of successive years as a proportion of one figure in the accounts. Such statements are normally prepared in relation to the balance sheet, relating each amount to the balance sheet totals. Thus for Barchester plc we can express the balance sheets for 19X7 and 19X8 as common size statements as follows:

	19X7		19X8	
Fixed assets		113		108
Current assets:				
Stock	40		49	
Debtors	23		26	
Cash	7		1	
	70		76	
Current liabilities:				
Trade creditors	6		14	
Proposed dividend	12		11	
Taxation	5		2	
Accruals	3		3	
	26		30	
Net current assets		44		46
		157		154
10% debenture		57		54
		100		100

The statement would normally cover a period of several years. This is a valuable tool for identifying changes in the way in which assets are employed and finance is obtained. Thus in this case we highlight the move from short-term to longer-term finance.

Funds flow statements

The funds statement is in itself a potentially valuable tool in the interpretation of accounts. This statement is a re-assortment of the data given in the profit and loss account and balance sheet, designed to give a view of the flow of resources through the business. SSAP 10 requires most limited companies to present a funds statement, but only lays down certain very broad principles relating to content; therefore, when comparing the funds statements of different companies it will often be necessary to restate the amounts in a common form of presentation. Having achieved a common form of presentation, it will be possible to make a comparison by using a common size statement.

As yet, there has not been established any form of common practice for the computation of accounting ratios derived from amounts shown in the funds statement. This is probably for two reasons:

1. Publication of the funds statement is a relatively recently established practice, and so there has not yet been time for a tradition of deriving accounting ratios to develop.
2. There is so much variety of practice in the presentation of funds statements that it would be difficult to predict what specific data will be available.

One value of the funds statement is that it does focus attention on the significance of movements in the resources of the business in absolute terms. For example, the reader of the funds statement of Barchester plc would observe from a glance at the funds statement that there had been a significant reduction in the overdraft and a significant inflow of funds raised from long-term borrowing.

Some authorities argue that there is considerable value in a cash-flow statement, focusing on cash rather than working capital movements. Advocates of this approach tend to see a particular value in the presentation of a cash-flow statement for each of several years, giving a view of overall trends.

Multivariate analysis

One way of using ratios is to identify several ratios which reflect on a particular aspect of a business and produce a single, combined, 'multivariate' ratio which represents some kind of weighted average. Most research in this field has focused on identifying liquidity problems, using ratios to identify companies that will have problems in meeting their obligations. The idea is that by weighting a number of ratios a 'Z' score is produced. By experience of firms in the industry that have become bankrupt, a score is then set below which bankruptcy is predicted. In practice, research studies that produce a useable 'Z' score rating to identify bankruptcy are marketed to customers on a fee-paying confidential basis.

Conclusion

In this chapter we have considered a range of techniques that help us consider a set of accounts.

Notes

7 Drawing conclusions

Introduction

We have considered in detail the computation and significance of a wide range of accounting ratios. The problem that remains is to decide how to draw together our conclusions from a study of accounting ratios, and present a meaningful report.

An approach

It would be misleading to claim that it is possible to establish a standard procedure for the interpretation of accounts in all situations. One major factor affecting any interpretation exercise is the amount of time, and other resources, available. This is clearly a major constraint for a student under examination conditions. It is important to remember that all users operate within certain resource constraints. In some cases these may be very restrictive. For example, a financial journalist may have to prepare brief comments on the accounts of a number of listed companies in time to meet a printing deadline the same day. In other cases, such as a bank considering a major loan proposal, it may be appropriate to devote very substantial resources to investigating financial data.

The following broad set of guidelines on tackling an interpretation problem is offered as an approach suitable to a user of accounts operating within strictly limited time constraints, particularly examination students:

1. Identify the interests of the user being served, and consider whether in consequence an emphasis should be put on any particular aspect of the affairs of the business.
2. Scrutinize the accounts for any apparent significant changes (e.g. large cash balance in previous year has become large overdraft in current year). Compute about half a dozen key ratios, covering liquidity, gearing and performance.
3. Consider ratios computed. Where there appear to be issues of interest raised, compute further ratios to probe and define these issues more thoroughly.

4. Summarize issues raised in brief notes, and consider interrelationships between issues raised.

5. Present a report in clear, simple, non-technical language. It is good practice to show how ratios have been computed in an appendix at the end of the report, so that the technical detail of computation does not clutter the report and obscure the issues raised. Conclusions must be drawn, but it is reasonable to make it clear that conclusions must in some cases be tentative. In some cases it might be valid to conclude that a specific line of further inquiry should be pursued.

It is important to emphasize that in this process it is vital that time be allowed for thinking and for presenting conclusions in a coherent manner.

We have seen how a wide range of detailed ratios can be computed for one company, Barchester plc. In practice, of course, we would be unlikely to find it necessary to compute all these ratios for the purpose of one ratio analysis exercise. We can illustrate the process of conducting a ratio analysis exercise by considering the example of Barchester plc.

Let us suppose that we have been asked to conduct this exercise by a client considering a purchase of shares in the company. For this purpose we will have to consider all aspects of the company's position, but with a special emphasis on performance.

Initial analysis

Our next stage is to glance quickly through the accounts. In particular, the funds flow statement shows the substantial bank decrease, leading to some concern over liquidity. On this basis we might compute the following selection of ratios:

	19X8	19X7
Current ratio	2.5	2.7
Liquidity ratio	0.9	1.2
Gearing (based on total funds)	46%	45%
After-tax return on equity	14.1%	19.8%
Pre-tax return on equity	21.8%	30.5%
Pre-tax return on total funds	14.8%	19.8%
Related: Asset turnover	1.18	1.14
Net profit %	12.5%	17.3%

(Note that all the ratios in this chapter have been previously computed in the text.)

This initial selection of ratios tells us that gearing has changed little, but that the decline in the two areas of liquidity and performance require further investigation.

Looking at liquidity

To investigate liquidity we would now take a closer look at the funds flow statement. We can see that new investment in fixed assets has been little more than depreciation for the year. Cash outflows are attributable to the increased working capital requirement. To investigate this we look at the following ratios which examine use of working capital:

	19X8	19X7
Sales increase	10%	
Days stock	136	120
Days debtors	44	40
Creditors turnover	15.4	36.5

We find that the company's working capital requirement has increased both because of the increased level of activity (shown by the sales increase) and relaxed working capital control (shown by days stock and days debtors). We also find that the decline in creditors turnover suggests that we are taking more than twice as long to pay our trade creditors.

Looking at performance

To investigate performance we would look at our secondary ratios, and observe that the decline in the net profit percentage is particularly significant. Accordingly we would compute the following ratios:

	19X8	19X7
Gross profit %	40%	42%
Distribution cost: Sales	20%	18.1%
Administration cost: Sales	7.5%	6.6%
Administration cost increase	25%	
Fixed asset turnover	2	1.8

We can now see that the ent profit percentage has been eroded by a combination of reduced gross profit margins, increased distribution costs and increased administration costs. We might have expected the improved fixed asset turnover to help compensate for this, but the benefits have largely been lost by relaxed working capital control.

The report

A report on Barchester plc might be presented as follows:

Overview
During 19X8 both liquidity and profitability have declined. The decline in liquidity seems to be largely due to relaxation in working capital control, and has resulted in a worrying reliance on extended trade credit. The decline in profitability results from all types of cost increasing faster than sales.

Liquidity

Declining liquidity is reflected in the sharp fall in cash funds and the falls in both the liquidity ratio and the current ratio. No new outside finance has been raised during the year, with the company relying on funds generated from operations. Working capital requirements have grown both because of a 10% increase in sales and relaxed control over stock and debtors. The creditors turnover ratio is down by more than half, suggesting that the company is delaying payments to suppliers for more than twice as long as in 19X7.

Performance

Although sales have increased by 10%, the profit earned on sales has dropped by almost 4%. Gross profit margins have fallen, while both distribution costs and administration expenses have risen in relation to sales. A slight improvement in asset turnover has not been sufficient to compensate for this decline.

Summary

The company needs to exercise tighter control over both working capital and expenses. Reliance on trade credit as a source of finance appears dangerously high, and it may be necessary to seek alternative sources of finance.

Conclusion

Ratio analysis is a tool to be used in assessing the position of a business. In this chapter we have considered a systematic approach to the analysis of a set of accounts which puts the emphasis on *using* rather than *computing* ratios.

Notes

8 A full example

Introduction

In this chapter we apply the ratio analysis techniques we have learnt to the example 'Crosby plc' shown in Appendix 2. This example includes a range of complications. Readers might find it useful to attempt each stage of the analysis procedure for themselves and then compare their own approach to that suggested here.

Identify the emphasis

For the purposes of this example we will imagine a question formulated as follows:

"Barland Bank became the bankers of Crosby plc on 30 November 19X3. As a financial adviser, you are required to advise the responsible manager on issues raised by the accounts for the year to 31 December 19X3."

This is a wide ranging brief, since an alert bank manager will want a full appreciation of a client's business. However, it does involve a particular interest in issues of gearing and liquidity.

Scrutinize the accounts

There is a substantial amount of interesting detail in these accounts. An initial review might identify the following as being of interest:

1. Earnings per share down by over a third. Thus a fairly detailed analysis of profitability seems necessary.
2. Current liabilities are down while a new long-term loan has appeared. This is explained by the extract from the Chairman's statement at the end of the notes to the accounts. Since the overdraft in 19X2 has been long recognized as an ongoing facility, and has now effectively been converted to a long-term loan, we would be wise to treat the 19X2 overdraft as a long-term liability when computing our ratios.

3. The audit report draws our attention to the company's failure to comply with SSAP 21 on lease agreements. The increase in plant hire costs shown in note 3 suggests an increased use of leasing. Failure to comply with SSAP 21 will distort both the gearing and the asset turnover ratios. This failure, taken to the point of incurring a qualified audit report, also suggests that the company directors see gearing as a sensitive issue.

These three points do not represent a comprehensive list of issues raised by the accounts. They are, however, three points which will have a major impact on our analysis.

Initial ratio computation

We have now identified a number of areas for inquiry. Table 8.1 shows a selection of ratios we might compute at this stage. Note how, following the initial review of the accounts, the bank overdraft in 19X2 has been treated as a long-term liability. Because of the sharp decline in earnings per share three different versions of the primary ratio are computed.

Interpreting the ratios

The fall in both the gearing ratio and the liquidity ratio suggests that a further investigation of the liquidity position is needed. Gearing has only risen slightly, but in view of the apparent increase in off balance sheet finance might still cause concern. A fall of 1.4% in the return on total funds has been magnified by the impact of gearing to affect the pre-tax return on equity by a drop of 3.1%, and has been further affected by tax factors to cause a 4.8% decline in the post-tax return on equity.

Investigating liquidity

Ratios to investigate working capital management are also shown in Table 8.1 under the heading 'Investigating liquidity'. The £36,000 increase in operating working capital appears to be entirely due to the 8.3% increase in turnover, with a slight tightening of credit control and little change in the management of working capital. To explain the change in liquidity we should look at:

1. The funds statement. Here we might note the £700,000 outflow of funds on new property.
2. The change in current liabilities. Here we might note the £200,000 instalment on the new loan repayable in the coming year.

Investigating performance

Table 8.1 also shows some of the ratios we might compute to investigate the drop in the return on total funds employed. Since asset turnover has

Table 8.1   Ratios computed for Crosby plc

Initial computation:

	19X3	19X2

Current ratio $\dfrac{1{,}295}{745} = 1.7$ | $\dfrac{1{,}274}{1{,}209 - 720} = 2.6$

Liquidity ratio $\dfrac{1{,}295 - 854}{745} = 0.6$ | $\dfrac{1{,}274 - 800}{1{,}209 - 720} = 1$

Gearing (total borrowings, preference shares as part of equity) $\dfrac{1{,}800 + 745}{3{,}290 + 1{,}800 + 745} = 44\%$ | $\dfrac{1{,}000 + 1{,}209}{3{,}265 + 1{,}000 + 1{,}209} = 40\%$

After-tax return on equity $\dfrac{230 - 35}{1{,}000 + 500 + 790} = 8.5\%$ | $\dfrac{337 - 35}{1{,}000 + 500 + 765} = 13.3\%$

Pre-tax return on equity $\dfrac{382 - 35}{1{,}000 + 500 + 790} = 15.2\%$ | $\dfrac{450 - 35}{1{,}000 + 500 + 765} = 18.3\%$

Returns on total funds $\dfrac{582}{3{,}290 + 1{,}800 + 745} = 10\%$ | $\dfrac{624}{3{,}265 + 1{,}000 + 1{,}209} = 11.4\%$

Related:

Asset turnover $\dfrac{5{,}200}{3{,}290 + 1{,}800 + 745} = 0.9$ | $\dfrac{4{,}800}{3{,}265 + 1{,}000 + 1{,}209} = 0.9$

Net profit % $\dfrac{582}{5{,}200} = 11.2\%$ | $\dfrac{624}{4{,}800} = 13\%$

Investigating liquidity:

Sales increase $\dfrac{5{,}200 - 4{,}800}{4{,}800} = 8.3\%$

Days stock $\dfrac{854}{3{,}952} \times 365 = 79 \text{ days}$ | $\dfrac{800}{3{,}600} \times 365 = 81 \text{ days}$

Days debtors $\dfrac{405}{5{,}200} \times 364 = 28 \text{ days}$ | $\dfrac{370}{4{,}800} \times 365 = 28 \text{ days}$

Creditors turnover $\dfrac{5{,}200}{180} = 29$ | $\dfrac{4{,}800}{170} = 28$

Investigating performance:

Gross profit % $\dfrac{1{,}248}{5{,}200} = 24\%$ | $\dfrac{1{,}200}{4{,}800} = 25\%$

Distribution: Sales $\dfrac{250}{5{,}200} = 4.8\%$ | $\dfrac{240}{4{,}800} = 5\%$

Administration: Sales $\dfrac{416}{5{,}200} = 8\%$ | $\dfrac{336}{4{,}800} = 7\%$

Administration increase $\dfrac{416 - 336}{336} = 24\%$

not changed, our investigation will focus on ratios relevant to the fall in the net profit percentage. We find two reasons for this fall:

1. The drop in the gross profit percentage. Apparently increase in turnover has been achieved at the expense of a costly drop in profit margins.
2. The increase of 24% in administration expenses. We would expect these to contain a high proportion of fixed costs, so that the increase from 7% to 8% of sales is worrying.

Taxation

The tax charge has risen although profit has fallen. Note 4 explains this in terms of reduced deferred tax timing differences. There is no note on the potential deferred tax liability, and the accounting policies note suggests a rather lax approach to applying SSAP 15. In view of the move from buying to leasing of plant, this warrants further investigation.

The report

A report on Crosby plc might read as follows:

Overview
This has been a year of declining operating profitability, magnified in its impact on shareholders both by tax factors and gearing. Liquidity has declined, and may be strained further by the need to make loan re-payments and possible future tax liabilities.

Performance
The decline in operating performance reflects a poorer return earned on sales. This is attributable to:

1. Declining gross profit margins
2. Rising administration costs.

Liquidity
Both the current ratio and the liquidity ratio show a decline. Major reasons for this are the £700,000 investment in property, which has not been supported by new outside finance, and the obligation to pay the first £200,000 instalment on the five-year loan. Although the conversion of the overdraft to a five-year loan has reduced the apparent level of current liabilities it has in fact placed a strain on liquidity because of the obligation to repay over five years.

Gearing
Although reported borrowings have only risen by 4% in relation to total funds there are two points which give concern:

1. The audit report highlights the failure to capitalize finance leases in accordance with SSAP 21. Increased hire charges suggest extensive use of leasing as a source of off balance sheet finance.

2.   The accounting policies note suggests a possible underprovision for deferred tax.

Recommendations
The company is likely to be seeking new finance in the near future. The bank would be well advised to insist on this client producing detailed information on leasing and potential deferred tax liabilities. Any future agreement on borrowing restrictions might also include a clause insisting on full recognition of lease obligations and deferred tax liabilities. Provision of new finance should also be made conditional on production of a business plan including provision for tackling the problem of declining gross margins and growing administration costs. Finally, in view of the increasing gearing level, the company might be encouraged to consider raising new equity finance.

Conclusion

This was a detailed and complex example. It could legitimately be approached in a number of ways. The example does illustrate the value of combining ratio analysis, funds flow analysis and a detailed examination of accounting practices.

Notes

Appendix 1 Accounts of Barchester plc

Barchester plc — Profit and loss account for the year ended 31 December 19X8

	19X8		19X7	
	£000	£000	£000	£000
Turnover		4,015		3,650
Cost of sales		2,409		2,117
Gross profit		1,606		1,533
Distribution costs	803		660	
Administration expenses	300		240	
		1,103		900
Operating profit		503		633
Interest		100		100
Profit before tax		403		533
Tax		143		186
Profit attributable to shareholders		260		347
Dividend		160		200
Retained profit		100		147

Barchester plc — Balance sheet as at 31 December 19X8

	19X8		19X7	
	£000	£000	£000	£000
Fixed assets				
Plant and machinery		2,000		1,980
Current assets				
Stock	900		696	
Debtors	480		400	
Cash	20		119	
	1,400		1,215	

Current liabilities

Trade creditors	260		100	
Proposed dividend	160		200	
Taxation	80		85	
Accruals	50		60	
	550		445	
Net current assets		850		770
		2,850		2,750
10% debenture		1,000		1,000
		1,850		1,750
Ordinary shares of £1		450		450
Retained profit		1,400		1,300
		1,850		1,750

During the year depreciation charged on plant was £100,000. There were no plant disposals.

Barchester plc — Funds flow statement for the year ended 31 December 19X8

	£000	£000
Sources		
Profit before tax		403
Adjustment for item not involving movement of funds:		
Depreciation		100
Generated from operations		503
Applications		
Plant purchase	120	
Tax paid	148	
Dividend paid	200	
		468
		35
Increase/(decrease) in working capital		
Stock increase	204	
Debtors increase	80	
Creditor increase	(160)	
Accrual decrease	10	
	134	
Bank decrease	(99)	
		35

Appendix 2 Accounts of Crosby plc

Crosby plc — Profit and loss account for the year ended 31 December 19X3

	Note	19X3 £000	19X3 £000	19X2 £000	19X2 £000
Turnover	2		5,200		4,800
Cost of sales	3		3,952		3,600
Gross profit			1,248		1,200
Distribution costs	3	250		240	
Administrative expenses	3	416		336	
			666		576
			582		624
Interest payable	3		200		174
Profit before taxation	3		382		450
Taxation	4		152		113
Profit attributable to shareholders			230		337
Dividends	5		205		205
Retained profit			25		232
Earnings per ordinary share			4.9p		7.5p

Crosby plc — Balance sheet as at 31 December 19X3

	Note	19X3 £000	19X3 £000	19X2 £000	19X2 £000
Fixed assets:					
Tangible assets	7		4,540		4,200
Current assets:					
Stocks	8	854		800	
Debtors	9	420		421	
Cash at bank		21		53	
		1,295		1,274	
Creditors — amounts falling due within one year	10	745		1,209	

Net current assets			550	65
Total assets less current liabilities			5,090	4,265
Creditors: amounts falling due after more than one year				
Debenture loan	11	1,000		1,000
Bank loan	11	800		—
			1,800	1,000
			3,290	3,265
Capital and reserves:				
Called-up share capital	12		2,000	2,000
Share premium			500	500
Profit and loss			790	765
			3,290	3,265

Crosby plc — Statement of source and application of funds for the year ended 31 December 19X3

	19X3		19X2	
	£000	£000	£000	£000
Profit before taxation		382		450
Adjustment for items not involving movement of funds:				
Depreciation		260		340
Profit on disposal of assets		(70)		—
Generated from operations		572		790
Other sources:				
Sale of plant and vehicles	170		—	
Bank loan	1,000		—	
		1,170		—
		1,742		790
Application of funds:				
Purchase of property	700		200	
Tax paid	113		184	
Dividend paid	205	(1,018)	205	(589)
		724		201
Increase/(decrease) in working capital:				
Increase in stock	54		120	
(Decrease) increase in debtors	(1)		97	
Increase in creditors and accruals	(17)	36	(15)	202
Movement in net liquid funds:				
Bank and cash	(32)		38	
Overdraft	720	688	(39)	(1)
		724		201

Crosby plc — Notes to the accounts

1 Accounting policies
Deferred taxation. The company's policy is only to provide for deferred taxation when there is reason to believe that amounts will become payable within the next two years.

(Details of other accounting policies are omitted.)

2 Turnover
Turnover represents the invoiced amount of goods sold and services provided during the year, stated net of Value Added Tax.

3 Profit

	19X3 £000	19X2 £000
Profit is shown after charging or crediting:		
Cost of sales:		
Depreciation	160	200
Hire of plant	180	40
Profit on disposal of assets	(60)	—
Other costs	3,572	3,360
	3,952	3,600
Distribution costs:		
Profit on disposal of plant	(10)	—
Depreciation	60	100
Hire of plant	30	—
Other	170	140
	250	240
Administrative costs:		
Auditors' remuneration	30	25
Depreciation	40	40
Other	346	271
	416	336
Interest payable:		
On bank loans and overdrafts and loans wholly repayable within five years	120	94
On other loans	80	80
	200	174

4 Taxation

	19X3 £000	19X2 £000
Corporation tax at 52%	152	113

If full provision had been made for the potential amount of deferred tax the tax charge for the year would have been increased by £40,000 (19X2 — £113,000).

5 Dividends

	19X3 £000	19X2 £000
Preference — paid	35	35
Ordinary — proposed	170	170
	205	205

6 Earnings per ordinary share

The calculation of earnings per ordinary share is based on earnings, after deducting preference dividends, of £195,000 (19X2 — £302,000) and on 4,000,000 ordinary shares, being the number of ordinary shares in issue during the year.

7 Tangible fixed assets

	Freehold land and buildings £000	*Plant and machinery* £000	*Motor vehicles* £000	*Total* £000
Cost:				
At 1 January 19X3	3,100	1,200	800	5,100
Additions	700	—	—	700
Disposals	—	(400)	(100)	(500)
At 31 December 19X3	3,800	800	700	5,300
Depreciation:				
At 1 January 19X3	—	500	400	900
Provided in year	—	120	140	260
Disposals	—	(300)	(100)	(400)
At 31 December 19X3	—	320	440	760
Net book amount 31.12.X3	3,800	480	260	4,540
Net book amount 1.1.X3	3,100	700	400	4,200

8 Stocks

	19X3 £000	19X2 £000
The main categories of stock are:		
Raw materials	215	225
Work-in-progress	212	181
Finished goods	427	394
	854	800

9 Debtors

	19X3 £000	19X2 £000
Trade debtors	405	370
Prepayments	15	51
	420	420

10 Creditors: amounts falling due within one year

	19X3	19X2
	£000	£000
Current instalment due on loan	200	—
Bank overdraft	—	720
Trade creditors	180	170
Corporation tax	152	113
Proposed dividend	170	170
Other creditors	25	20
Accruals	18	16
	745	1,209

11 Loans

	19X3	19X2
	£000	£000
Not wholly repayable within five years	1,000	1,000
Wholly repayable within five years	1,000	—
	2,000	1,000
Amounts due within one year (included in current liabilities)	200	—
	1,800	1,000

12 Share capital

	19X3	19X2
	No.	No.
Authorized, issued, and fully paid:		
Ordinary shares at 25p	4,000,000	4,000,000
3.5% preference shares of £1	1,000,000	1,000,000

Extract from the chairman's statement

Over the years your company has become reliant on an overdraft facility, which has been regularly renewed. Both your directors and the company's bankers have become concerned at this position, and on 1 January 19X3 the bank agreed to make the company a loan of £1,000,000 at 12% interest, repayable in five equal annual instalments commencing from 31 March 19X4.

Auditors' report to the members of Crosby plc

We have audited the financial statements on pages 1 to 6 in accordance with approved Auditing Standards.

The company has failed to comply with SSAP 21 *Accounting for Leases and Hire Purchase Contracts*, choosing to treat all leases as operating leases, and not disclosing details of future commitments.

Except for the above in our opinion the financial statements give a true and fair view of the state of the company's affairs at 31 December 19X3 and of the profit and source and application of funds for the year then ended and comply with the Companies Act 1985.

Palliser & Co
Chartered Accounts
15 June 19X4

Improving examination performance on financial analysis

Throughout this text we have considered analytical techniques from the point of view of the exam candidate as well as the practitioner. Ratio analysis is a particularly difficult exam topic because of the 'open ended' nature of a complete answer — the student may well spot implications in the question that the examiner has not spotted himself.

The first and most important piece of advice, therefore, is to practise. That is why over half this book is devoted to examples! Practice enables you to become familiar with the wide range of ways in which exam questions can be set.

Next, if you are sitting an external exam, study old question papers and any official model answers provided. This will give you an insight into how your examiner approaches the topic. However, don't rely on this too much — the examiner may change!

Similarly, in an internal exam, note carefully the way your teacher uses terminology and expect to find this reflected in the exam.

If you find a term you have never heard before used in the exam, don't panic. The chances are that your competitors have the same problem. Think carefully about the words used and their context to spot the likely meaning.

You may be asked for a ratio which can mean several different things, such as 'return on capital employed'. Do two things:

1. Think which ratio is the most sensible to use in the context of the question.
2. Write a note in your answer explaining why you have chosen that definition.

Finally, go into the exam with a procedure for tackling 'open ended' questions along the lines suggested in Chapter 7.

Remember that by having taken the trouble to go through a book of this kind you have put yourself amongst the best prepared candidates. Tackle the exam with confidence.

Good luck!

Questions 1 to 38

Question 1

Ratio analysis is an important technique in the understanding of company accounts.

(i)   What is ratio analysis?
(ii) What standards can be used to compare ratios?
(iii) What are the problems involved in producing useful and meaningful
(iv) ratios?
     Give one example of:
     (a) a liquidity ratio,
     (b) a profitability ratio,
     (c) an investment ratio,
     and show how each is calculated.

(SCCA, PI, May 1983)

Question 2

Discuss the significance to investors of:

(a) equity yield;
(b) price-earnings ratio; and
(c) dividend cover.

(SCCA, P4, May 1983)

Question 3

Riverside plc and Orlando plc are companies engaged in the same kind of business in the United Kingdom. The business is cyclical and, from past experience, profits before deducting loan interest are liable to fluctuate up to 50% above or below the 1982 level.
   The following information is provided for 1982:

	Riverside	Orlando
	£000	£000
Ordinary share capital		
(£1 shares)	2,000	1,000
Reserves (average figure for 1982)	1,500	1,000
15% debentures repayable 1990–95	500	4,000
Profit for 1982 before deducting loan interest	600	900

Required:

(a) Calculations for each company of the rate of return on shareholders' equity.
(b) A discussion of the capital structure of each company from the viewpoint of the shareholders and management. The discussion should include calculations of the possible variations in the rate of return earned for the shareholders.

(AIB, April 1983)

Question 4

The following information is provided relating to the affairs of two companies engaged in similar trading activities:

	A Ltd	B Ltd
Ordinary share capital	£800,000	£500,000
15% debentures	£200,000	£500,000

Each company earned a trading profit before finance charges of 110,000 in year 1 and £190,000 in year 2.

Corporation tax is charged at 50% on the trading profits after finance charges have been deducted.

The company pays out as dividends its entire after-tax profits.

Required:

(a) Summary profit and loss accounts, dealing with the results of each of the two ccompanies' activities during year 1 and year 2, so far as the information given above permits.
(b) Calculations of after-tax profits, expressed as percentages of ordinary share capital for each company in respect of both year 1 and year 2.
(c) A discussion of the returns earned for shareholders over the two-year period.

(AIB, April 1979)

Question 5

Forest Ltd and Beechwood Ltd are companies trading in a similar range of products in different geographical areas. Each company prepares its accounts on the calendar year basis and the following information is provided in respect of 1981:

Summarized balance sheets at 31 December 1981

	Forest Ltd	Beechwood Ltd
	£000	£000
Issued share capital	1,000	500
Reserves	500	500
	1,500	1,000
12% debenture stock	500	2,000
	2,000	3,000
Current liabilities	400	600
	2,400	3,600
Gross assets	2,400	3,600

Profit and loss account extracts

	Forest Ltd	Beechwood Ltd
	£000	£000
Sales	7,400	7,000
Operating profit	400	600
Less: Debenture interest	60	240
Net profit	340	360

Required:

A full discussion of the financial results achieved by each of the two companies based on the following financial ratios:

(i)   profit percentage (operating profit as a percentage of sales);
(ii)   asset turnover (sales to capital employed);
(iii) percentage return on capital employed;
(iv) percentage return on long-term funds;
(v)   percentage return on shareholders' equity.

Notes:

For the purpose of this question capital employed is defined as gross assets. You should show clearly the calculation of each of the financial ratios.

(AIB, April 1982)

Question 6

The following are the summarized revenue accounts and balance sheets of Aix Limited.

Revenue accounts for years ended 31 December

	1978		1979	
		£ thousands		
Sales		800		1,100
Less: Opening stock	110		130	
Costs of production	500		700	
Closing stock	(130)		(170)	
Cost of goods sold	480		660	
Running expenses (including interest charges)	260	740	362	1,022
Net profit		60		78
Proposed dividend		—		40
Retained profit		60		38

Balance sheets as at 31 December

	1978		1979
		£ thousands	
Ordinary share capital		200	200
Retained profit		100	138
12% debentures, issued 1 January 1979		—	200
Bank overdraft		10	—
Dividends		—	40
Creditors		110	120
		420	698
Fixed assets		170	338
Stock		130	170
Debtors		120	160
Bank		—	30
		420	698

No dividends were paid during either 1978 or 1979.

Required:

(a) A calculation of the following accounting ratios and percentages for 1978 and 1979 presented in the following tabular format:

	1978	1979
Liquid ratio		
Average rate of stock turnover		
Net profit as a percentage of sales		
Earnings as a percentage of long-term capital employed		
Net earnings for ordinary shareholders as a percentage of equity		
Ratio of sales to long-term capital employed		

For the purpose of your calculations equity and long-term capital employed are to be included at their estimated figures at 30 June in each year, assuming no seasonal variations in the level of business activity.
(b) Comments on the implications of the differences between the above ratios and percentages between the two years.

Note:
Ignore taxation.

(AIB, April 1980)

Question 7

Maximon Ltd is a well-established company engaged in the manufacture and sale of metal products. The following information is obtained from the company's financial records.

Balance sheet at 30 June

	£	£	£	£
Fixed assets at cost		637,100		767,300
Less: Depreciation		297,500		321,400
		339,600		445,900
Trade investments at cost		106,000		106,000
Current assets:				
Stock and work-in-progress	230,200		260,100	
Trade debtors and prepayments	135,800		196,400	
Bank balance	—		9,300	
	366,000		465,800	
Less: current liabilities:				
Trade creditors and accruals	96,800		101,700	
Taxation due: 31.3.82	63,800		—	
31.3.83	—		61,000	
Dividend payable	60,000		66,000	
Bank overdraft	71,000		—	
	291,600		228,700	
Net current assets		74,400		237,100
		£520,000		£789,000
Financed by:				
Ordinary share capital				
(Ordinary shares of £1 each)		200,000		220,000
Share premium account		—		30,000
Reserves		320,000		339,000
		520,000		589,000
15% debenture		—		200,000
		£520,000		£789,000

Profit and loss accounts year ended 30 June

	1981 £	1982 £
Operating profit	160,500	176,000
Less: Finance charges — bank interest	9,200	—
— debenture interest	—	30,000
Net profit before taxation	151,300	146,000
Less: Taxation	63,800	61,000
Profit after taxation	87,500	85,000
Less: Dividend proposed	60,000	66,000
Retained profit for the year	£27,500	£19,000

Notes:
1. On 31 January 1982 a rights issue was made of one ordinary share for every ten ordinary shares currently held. For the purpose of this issue the ordinary shares were valued at £2.50 each.
2. The debenture is secured on the company's freehold property which is included amongst fixed assets in the balance sheet shown above.
3. During the year ended 30 June 1982, the company disposed of fixed assets which cost £65,200 some years ago for £17,900. A loss of £9,600 arising on disposal has been deducted in arriving at operating profit for the year.

Required:
(a) The statement of source and application of funds of Maximon Ltd, at 30 June 1981 and 30 June 1982, in accordance with the provisions contained in Statement of Standard Accounting Practice No. 10 entitled 'Statements of Source and Application of Funds'.
(b) An examination of the respective financial positions of Maximon Ltd at 30 June 1981 and 30 June 1982 and a discussion of the financial developments which have occurred during the intervening period. The financial statement prepared under (a) and relevant accounting ratios should be used to support your analysis.

Note:
Ignore advance corporation tax.

(AIB, September 1982)

Question 8

Unigear Ltd is a high-fashion retail trading company with an issued share capital of £200,000 in ordinary shares.

The detailed profit and loss account for the year ended 31 December 1972 showed the following:

	1971			1972	
£	£			£	£
	1,500,000	Sales			1,000,000
		Less: Cost of sales:			
250,000		Opening stock		300,000	
950,000		Purchases		760,000	
1,200,000				1,060,000	
300,000		*Less:* Closing stock		410,000	
	900,000				650,000
	600,000				350,000
		Deduct:			
10,450		Rent and rates		12,106	
3,608		Light and heat		4,942	
609		Telephone		71	
301,459		Wages and salaries		212,374	
40,216		Advertising		42,605	
2,600		Repairs and renewals		750	
4,224		Bad debts		12,943	
22,328		Bank interest and commission		46,420	
850		Audit fee		1,000	
5,960		General expenses		7,240	
2,400		Depreciation		2,000	
	394,704				343,098
	205,296	Trading profit for year			6,902
		Deduct:			
	55,000	Corporation tax			5,500
	150,296	Profit for year after taxation			1,402
	40,000	*Less:* Dividend			—
	110,296				1,402
	24,843	*Add:* Balance brought forward			135,139
	£135,139	Balance carried forward			£136,541

Wages and salaries include directors' remuneration of £24,650 (1971 — £67,740) and the charge for corporation tax in the year to 31 December 1972 includes an underprovision of £2,500 relating to the previous year.

You are required to write a short report to the directors giving your observations on the results for the year and the comparison with the previous year.

(ICAEW, September 1973)

Question 9

The following is an extract from *Accountancy*, March 1977, p. 50:

'Take profit before tax divided by current liabilities; current assets as a proportion of total liabilities; current liabilities as proportion of total tangible assets; take into account the no-credit interval; mix them in the right proportions and you can tell whether a company will go bust.'

The no-credit interval is defined as (Current assets − Current liabilities) ÷ (Operating costs excluding Depreciation).

The following are the summarized accounts of Go-go Products Ltd and Numerous Inventions Ltd for the years ended 30 April 1977 and 1976.

| | Go-go Products | | Numerous Inventions | |
| | 1977 | 1976 | 1977 | 1976 |
	£	£	£	£
Turnover	30,067	25,417	9,734	8,044
Costs:				
Depreciation	311	284	331	195
Other	28,356	24,198	8,313	6,571
Profit before tax	1,400	935	1,090	1,278
	30,067	25,417	9,734	8,044
Intangible assets	918	937	—	—
Fixed assets	4,644	5,228	1,950	1,530
Stock	6,243	6,773	986	1,257
Debtors	4,042	4,580	3,234	2,236
Bank	516	184	2,578	1,366
	16,363	17,702	8,748	6,389
Creditors	5,261	5,144	1,297	972
Current taxation	312	379	483	321
Short-term borrowing	2,357	4,447	2,577	1,174
Long-term loans	1,409	1,168	55	38
Capital and reserves	7,024	6,564	4,336	3,884
	16,363	17,702	8,748	6,389

You are required to:

(a) Calculate three of the stated factors for the two companies and two others you consider relevant to their going-concern status.
(b) Compare the two companies stating clearly which of your calculated ratios have moved in an unfavourable direction; and
(c) Describe and discuss the limitations of ratio analysis as a predictor of failure.

(ICAEW, July 1977)

Question 10

Summarized accounts of New Ideas Limited as shown below:

Balance sheet on 30 April 1976

| | 1976 | 1975 |
	£000	£000
Fixed assets (net)	6,401	2,519

Current assets:

Stock	25,426	20,231
Debtors	21,856	20,264
Balance at bank	2,917	6,094
	56,600	49,108
Ordinary shares of 50p	5,000	5,000
Revenue reserves	14,763	12,263
Deferred taxation	5,433	3,267

Loans:

10% debenture 1995/1999	10,000	10,000

Current liabilities:

Creditors	18,762	16,431
Taxation	1,642	1,247
Dividends	1,000	900
	56,000	49,108

Results for the year ended 30 April 1976

	1976	1975
	£000	*£000*
Sales	264,626	220,393
Trading profit	9,380	8,362
Interest payable	1,000	1,000
Taxation	4,380	3,642
Dividend	1,500	1,400

1. The ordinary shares are quoted at £1.20.
2. New Ideas Limited requires £16 million for an investment project and is considering one of the following:
    (i)   the issue to shareholders of £16 million 10% convertible (£1 for 1 share) debentures 1990 at par;
    (ii) a rights issue at 80p, or
    (iii) the sale in the market of £16 million 13% debentures 1990/2000 at par.

You are required to:

(a) Calculate from the balance sheet and results:
    (i)   two ratios particularly significant to creditors;
    (ii) two ratios particularly significant to management; and
    (iii) two ratios particularly significant to shareholders.
(b) Comment briefly upon the change between 1975 and 1976 in the ratios you have calculated.
(c) Calculate the immediate effect of the three schemes upon the gearing (or leverage) ratio.
(d) Calculate the effect of the three schemes on the earnings per share on the assumption that the 1976 profits from the existing assets will be maintained and that the £16 million new investment will produce £3.5 million profit before interest and tax at 50%; and

(e)   Briefly advise the management on the most appropriate method to
      use.

(*ICAEW, July 1976*)

Question 11

Summarized balance sheet, profit and loss account and statement of source
and application of funds for Northern Manufacturing Co Ltd follow.

	31 December	
	1979	*1978*
	£000	*£000*
Balance sheet		
Fixed assets	1,900	1,400
Current assets:		
Stocks	1,000	600
Debtors	800	500
Cash	—	40
	3,700	2,540
Share capital:		
Ordinary shares of £1	1,000	600
Reserves	600	300
Convertible 8% loan	500	500
12% loan repayable 1990	600	600
Current liabilities:		
Trade creditors	700	350
Overdraft	300	190
	3,700	2,540
Profit and loss account		
Turnover	7,000	5,000
Trading profit, before depreciation	800	500
Depreciation	600	400
Advance corporation tax paid and written off	60	33
Dividends paid, as interim and only one for year	140	67
Retained	—	—
Statement of source and application of funds		
Profit before taxation and depreciation	800	500
Share issues	700	—
Increase in creditors	350	100
	1,850	600
Purchase of plant	1,100	200
Dividends paid	140	67
Advance corporation tax paid and written off	60	33

Increase in debtors	300	100
Increase in stock	400	200
	2,000	600
Increase (decrease) in net bank and cash balance	(150)	—

The overdraft has been renewed every three months since 1 January 1970. Since that time the maximum overdraft each year has varied between £750,000 and £250,000.

The 8% loan is convertible into ordinary shares at the rate of one ordinary share for each £1 of loan stock on 31 December 1985.

There was an issue of new shares to existing shareholders on the basis of four new shares for every six held at a price of £1.75 each on 1 May 1979.

The 1979 accounts were published on 31 May 1980 and since that date the share price has fluctuated between £2.00 and £1.10 The current price is £1.80.

No taxation is provided as planned expansion of activities indicates that none will be payable in the foreseeable future.

You are required to:

(a) Calculate earnings per share as disclosed in the accounts of 1978 and 1979.
(b) Calculate the current P/E ratio and the range of the ratio since 31 May 1980.
(c) Calculate three ratios based on the accounts of 1978 and 1979 appropriate to an assessment of the liquidity of the company, and
(d) Comment on the liquidity position of the company at 31 December 1979.

(ICAEW, July 1980)

Question 12

There are given below the activities of eight companies, and information from the companies' balance sheets expressed as percentages of net assets employed.

You are required to state, with reasons, which balance sheet you consider identifies with each of the companies. Marks will be allotted for reasons only and not for the matching of correct pairs.

The respective areas of activity of the companies are:

A. General engineering
B. Investment in properties for rental
C. Estate development and house builders
D. Whisky distillers and blenders
E. Brewers
F. Retail stores
G. Conglomerate with various activities
H. Insurance brokers.

The assets and current liabilities shown as percentage of net assets employed are:

Reference	1	2	3	4	5	6	7	8
	%	%	%	%	%	%	%	%
Land and property	83	31	2	32	72	81	11	147
Other fixed assets	13	28	3	22	23	7	9	3
Stock and work-in-progrss	8	43	111	45	—	11	75	—
Trade debtors	11	36	36	56	436	4	18	7
Cash/temporary investments	4	5	1	3	91	7	1	1
	119	143	153	158	622	110	114	158
Trade creditors	(19)	(34)	(35)	(47)	(509)	(10)	(9)	(9)
Bank overdraft	(—)	(9)	(18)	(11)	(13)	(—)	(5)	(49)
Net assets employed	100	100	100	100	100	100	100	100

(ICMA)

Question 13

The capital structures of Alpha Ltd and of Gamma Ltd at 30 June 1979 were as follows:

	Alpha Ltd	Gamma Ltd
	£	£
8% debenture stock	—	600,000
9% (now 6.3% + tax credit) preference shares of £1	1,800,000	900,000
Ordinary shares of 25p	900,000	300,000
Reserves	300,000	1,200,000
	3,000,000	3,000,000

Both companies had profits of £800,000 before debenture interest and tax for the year ended 30 June 1979 and anticipate an increase of 12½% for the year ending 30 June 1980.

Required:

1. Define gearing in relation to the capital structure of a company and outline the significant effects thereof.
2. Explain what you understand by the term 'concealed gearing' and give two examples.
3. State, with reasons, which of the two companies you consider to be the more highly geared.

(ICAS, August 1979)

Question 14

A statistical survey showed the following comparison of financial ratios for the dairy-food retailing and building materials industries:

	Dairy food retailing	Building materials
Price earnings ratio (nil basis)	9.00	7.00
Dividend yield	4.50%	6.50%
Stock/turnover	0.8 months	3.0 months
Pre-tax return on capital employed	23.00%	16.00%

Required:

1. Explain the meaning of the above ratios.
2. Give your views on the principal reasons for the variations in each of the ratios between the two industries.

(*ICAS, April 1980*)

Question 15

The following is a summary of the latest accounts of a listed company:

Profit and loss account for the year ended 31 March 1982

	£000	£000
Trading profit		6,800
Investment income		100
		6,900
Interest paid		1,000
Profit before tax and extraordinary items		5,900
UK corporation tax	1,010	
Irrecoverable advance corporation tax	500	
		1,540
Profit before extraordinary items		4,360
Extraordinary items net of taxation		480
		3,880
Dividends		3,500
Retained profit for year		380

Balance sheet as at 31 March 1982

	£000
Fixed assets	42,200
Current assets	8,700
	50,900
Less: Current liabilities	7,300
	43,600
Financed by:	
Ordinary capital: 15,000,000 shares of £1 each	15,000
Reserves	18,600
Debentures	10,000
	43,600

The company's ordinary shares of £1 each were quoted at £2.20 each on 30 June 1982.

Required:

1. Calculate the P/E ratio and the dividend yield at 30 June 1982.
2. Discuss briefly the significance to potential investors of the P/E ratio and the dividend yield.
3. Explain why it might be considered desirable to disclose in the financial statements the earnings per share on both the nil and the net basis.

(ICAS, September 1982)

Question 16

Your client Ballindine Ltd is a manufacturer of wallpaper. At the commencement of the audit you are presented with the draft accounts together with the budgeted figures for the year and the actual figures for the previous year. These are summarized below.

You are required to present an analysis of the changes planned in the budget and the changes which have actually occurred, consider a possible explanation for these changes, and state how this analytical review of the accounts might affect the conduct of your audit.

Profit and loss accounts:

	Year to: 31.12.82 Actual £000	Year to: 31.12.83 Budgeted £000	Year to: 31.12.83 Actual £000
Sales	600	800	700
Less: Cost of sales:			
Stock b/fwd	30	30	30
Purchases and manufacturing costs	360	510	450
	390	540	480
Stock c/fwd	30	60	60
	360	480	420
Gross profit	240	320	280
Less: Expenses:			
Salaries	70	80	80
Transport and general exp.	40	55	50
Rental rates	20	30	24
Advertising	20	60	60
Depreciation	20	40	40
Interest	—	—	3
	170	265	257
Net profit	70	55	23
Retained profit b/fwd	10	80	80
Retained profit c/fwd	80	125	103

Balance sheets:

Fixed assets at written-down value:			
Land and buildings	100	100	180
Plant	50	120	120
	150	220	300
Current assets:			
Stock	30	60	60
Debtors	50	100	100
Bank	50	—	—
	130	160	160
Current liabilities:			
Creditors	30	60	60
Bank overdraft	—	15	67
	30	75	127
Net current assets	100	85	33
	250	305	333
Share capital — £1 ordinary shares	150	150	150
Share premium	20	20	20
Retained profits	80	135	103
	205	305	273
10% debentures — secured	—	—	60
	250	305	333

(AIA)

Question 17

GIV Manufacturing Ltd is an old-established light engineering company whose shares are listed on the Stock Exchange. The management feels content with the company's general performance but the share price has not performed well over the last two years.

The key ratios for the company are given below:

Ratios:	1976	1977	1978	1979	1980
Liquidity:					
Current	2.0	2.1	2.0	2.3	2.5
Liquid	1.1	1.1	1.0	1.1	1.3
Leverage:					
% of total long-term finance which is fixed	38	32	28	23	16
Times fixed interest covered	8.4	9.6	10.2	12.2	14.4
Efficiency:					
Debtors (days)	35	34	42	48	54
Creditors (days)	40	39	40	41	40
Inventory (days)	60	58	54	62	68

Profitability — % of net worth:

Company	35	30	30	28	26
Industry	25	25	25	25	25

Sales index:

Company	100	120	160	180	185
Industry	100	110	120	135	150

Dividend payout %

Company	20	20	20	20	20
Industry	40	40	40	40	40

Share price index:

Company	100	150	200	160	130
Industry	100	100	130	120	110

Requirement:

You are required to examine these ratios and write a report to the finance director of GIV Manufacturing Ltd on the financial strategy of the company during the five-year period 1976–80 commenting in particular on:

(a)   the company's management of working capital; and
(b)   the possible reasons for the trend in the company's share price.

(ICAI, PE, II, Summer 1981)

Question 18

The Karri-Krane Company is in business as a manufacturer and distributor of a range of mechanical handling systems. Three years ago it undertook a major plant expansion programme which was intended to give it the extra capacity needed to exploit new export markets and the cost was funded by an issue of loan stock to the public. Its subsequent performance has been severely criticized by City editors and by institutional investment managers who supported the issue and this has led to the resignation of the chief executive.

You are required to assume that you are on a short-list of candidates who are being considered for the vacant post. To assist the chairman in making his final selection, he has asked you to study the trading record and the balance sheets of the company over the five-year period 1974–8, as set out below, and to submit a short report giving your analysis of its performance from your own interpretation of the figures.

In preparing your report you should give particular attention to assessing the company's profitability and its use of financial resources by reference to commonly accepted performance indicators and ratios. You may make any reasonable assumptions based on the figures to point to possible remedial measures, but your comments should be relevant to this approach and you should avoid generalized statements that are unsupported by your financial appraisal. Marks will be awarded accordingly.

	1978	1977	1976	1975	1974
	£000	*£000*	*£000*	*£000*	*£000*
Sales	£23,500	£21,000	£19,000	£16,800	£15,000

	£000	£000	£000	£000	£000
Trading profit	2,100	1,600	2,100	1,700	1,350
Less:					
Loan interest	356	356	226	96	96
Taxation	870	620	930	800	620
Dividends	525	525	525	525	525
Undistributed profit	349	99	419	279	109

Balance sheets					
	1978	1977	1976	1975	1974
Land and buildings	5,300	5,300	5,100	3,250	3,300
Plant and machinery, etc.	3,700	3,300	3,250	2,700	2,500
	9,000	8,600	8,350	5,950	5,800
Stocks	3,500	3,000	2,800	2,300	2,000
Debtors	5,900	4,700	3,700	2,800	2,500
Bank	—	—	375	725	825
	9,400	7,700	6,875	5,825	5,325
Creditors	3,400	2,700	2,300	1,900	1,700
Taxation	700	600	700	550	500
Dividend	325	325	325	325	325
Bank overdraft	1,275	475	—	—	—
	5,700	4,100	3,325	2,775	2,525
Net current assets	3,700	3,600	3,550	3,050	2,800
Total net assets	£12,700	£12,200	£11,900	£9,000	£8,600
Share capital:					
Ordinary shares	5,250	3,500	3,500	3,500	3,500
Reserves	3,200	4,600	4,500	4,080	3,800
Deferred taxation	1,450	1,300	1,100	620	500
Loan capital:					
12% Loan stock 1985–8	800	800	800	800	800
13% Loan stock 1996–8	2,000	2,000	2,000	—	—
Total funds employed	£12,700	£12,200	£11,900	£9,000	£8,600

Notes:

1. A-one-for-two scrip issue was made in 1978 by transfer from Reserves.
2. Land and buildings and plant and machinery are stated at cost, less depreciation provided to date.

(Cert. Dip. F.A., December 1978)

Question 19

Tapsave Ltd is a manufacturer of machine tools, and is at present contemplating an issue of £2,000,000 10% debenture stock (1995–8) in order to assist the remodelling of its present production facilities. Some shareholders are reluctant to approve additional long-term debt due to the fact that the machine tools industry is subject to wide-ranging fluctuations in sales and profits. A group of shareholders have approached you and asked you to comment on the performance of Tapsave Ltd as compared with the industrial averages, and to make a recommendation as to whether they should approve the proposed additional long-term debt.

Abbreviated financial statements and typical ratios for firms in the machine tools industry are as follows:

Tapsave Ltd: Profit and loss accounts for the years ended 31 December 1978 and 1977

	1978	1978	1977	1977
	£000	£000	£000	£000
Sales		23,500		20,500
Cost of goods sold		16,000		14,000
Gross profit		7,500		6,500
	£000		£000	
Selling expenses	2,000		1,900	
Administration expenses	3,000		2,600	
		5,000		4,500
Net operating profit		2,500		2,000
Interest		500		300
Net profit before taxation		2,000		1,700
Taxation		1,200		1,020
Net profit after taxation		800		680
Undistributed profits b/f		6,090		5,690
		6,890		6,370
Dividends paid		525		280
Undistributed profits c/f		£6,365		£6,090

Balance sheets as at 31 December 1978 and 1977

	1978	1978	1977	1977
	£000	£000	£000	£000
Fixed assets (net)		6,315		5,600
Other assets		800		750
		7,115		6,350
Current assets:	£000		£000	
Prepaid expenses	100		100	
Stock	5,100		3,200	
Debtors (net)	2,900		1,900	
Cash and bank	600		590	
	8,700		5,790	
Less: Current liabilities	3,600		2,400	
		5,100		3,390
		£12,215		£9,740
Represented by:		£000		£000
Ordinary 50p shares authorized and issued fully paid		350		350

Undistributed profits	6,365	6,090
	6,715	6,440
8% Debenture stock (1987–9)	5,500	3,300
	£12,215	£9,740

Typical industrial ratios for 1978 and 1977

Gross profit to sales	34%
Current ratio	2.5:1
Acid test ratio	1.2:1
Average age of debtors	30 days
Stock turnover	5 times
Interest earned	8 times
Debt/equity ratio	0.70:1
Net profit before tax to net assets	19.5%

You are required to:

(a) Compute the above ratios for Tapsave Ltd for both 1976 and 1977 taking into account the stock valuation at 31 December 1976 of £2,500,000 and the debtors' balance at the same date of £1,700,000.
(b) Comment on the performance of Tapsave Ltd and recommend a course of action to the group of shareholders.

(Cert. Dip. F.A. June 1979)

Question 20

The financial director of Peak Canning Co Ltd has recently examined the financial statements for 1973 to 1975, and concluded that the present level of sales cannot be continued without an increase in borrowing. He has requested you to make an analysis of the firm's financial position in the light of the industrial averages and to advise him of the firm's strengths and weaknesses.

Peak Canning Co Ltd
Balance sheets as at 31 December

	1973		1974		1975	
Fixed assets:						
Land and buildings		£61,200		£163,200		£153,000
Machinery		188,700		147,900		127,500
Other fixed assets		35,700		10,200		7,600
		285,600		321,300		288,100
Current assets:						
Stock	328,500		637,500		1,032,800	
Debtors	306,000		346,800		484,500	
Cash	76,500	765,000	35,700	1,020,000	25,500	1,542,800
		£1,050,600		£1,341,300		£1,830,900

Ordinary share capital		459,000		459,000		459,000
Undistributed profits		351,900		438,600		489,600
		810,900		897,600		948,600
Long-term loan (mortage)		56,100		51,000		45,900
Current liabilities						
Accruals	61,200		71,400		96,900	
Creditors	122,400		193,800		382,500	
Bank overdraft	—		127,500		357,000	
		183,600		392,700		836,400
		£1,050,600		£1,341,300		£1,830,900

Peak Canning Co Ltd
Income statement for the year ending 31 December

		1973		1974		1975
Net sales		£3,315,000		£3,442,500		£3,570,000
Less: Cost of goods sold		2,652,000		2,754,000		2,856,000
Gross operating profit		663,000		688,500		714,000
General administrative and selling expenses	255,000		280,500		306,000	
Depreciation	102,000		127,500		153,000	
Miscellaneous expenses	51,000		107,100		153,000	
		408,000		515,100		612,000
Net income before tax		255,000		173,400		102,000
Corporation tax (50%)		127,500		86,700		51,000
Net income after tax		£127,500		£86,700		£51,000

Canning industry ratios (1975)**

Quick ratio	1.0
Current ratio	2.7
Stock turnover*	7.0×
Average collection period	32 days
Fixed asset turnover*	13.0
Total asset turnover*	2.6×
Return on total assets	19.0%
Return on net worth	36.0%
Debt ratio	50.0%
Profit margin on sales	7.0%

(*Based on year end balance sheet figures. **Industry average ratios have been constant for the past three years.)

You are required to:

(a) Calculate the key financial ratios for Peak and compare with the industrial averages.
(b) State the strengths and weaknesses revealed by the ratio analysis.

(Cert. Dip. F. A., 1976)

Question 21

Your Uncle Herbert sends you a copy of the accounts of two companies in which he owns shares, both retail stores, Cotton Value plc and Engels & Althorpe plc. Extracts are attached. He is puzzled because the latest share prices at October 1981 are:

Cotton Value plc	£0.45
Engels & Althorpe plc	£1.15

although Cotton Value plc shows higher earnings per share.

You are required to prepare notes of your views as to the reasons which might explain this situation.

Balance sheets

	Cotton Value plc				Engels & Althorpe plc			
	31.1.81		31.1.80		31.1.81		31.1.80	
	£m	£m	£m	£m	£m	£m	£m	£m
Fixed assets		530		513		676		638
Current assets:								
Stock	195		195		116		109	
Debtors	41		31		43		33	
Bank and cash	17		6		109		45	
	253		232		268		187	
Current liabilities:								
Creditors	96		91		140		98	
Bank loans	73		57		50		31	
Taxation	9		7		80		78	
Proposed dividend	13		13		30		25	
	191		168		300		232	
Net current assets/(liabilities)		62		64		(32)		(45)
		592		577		644		593
Ordinary shares of 25p		95		95		326		326
Revenue reserves		483		470		270		219
		578		565		596		545
Loans		14		12		48		48
		592		577		644		593

Profit and loss accounts

	Cotton Value plc				Engels & Althorpe plc			
	31.1.81		31.1.80		31.1.81		31.1.80	
	£m	£m	£m	£m	£m	£m	£m	£m
Turnover		952		888		1873		1668
Profit before interest		53		65		184		178
Interest paid:								
Short term	13		8		9		7	
Long term	1		1		3		3	
	14		9		12		10	

Less interest received	1		1		9		5	
	13		8		3		5	
Profit before taxation	40		57		181		173	
Taxation	9		16		80		80	
	31		41		101		93	
Dividends	18		18		50		45	
Retained profit	13		23		51		48	
Earnings per share	8.2p		10.8p		7.7p		7.1p	

Question 22

In 1898 the Silverbridge Working Men's Club was founded. The club still survives in the same premises. During 1988 the club was refurbished and refitted. However, the 1988 accounts showed a loss so that at the AGM held in February 1989 an entirely new committee was elected. Your friend Albert, the Chairman of the new committee, is now due to present the 1989 accounts to the 1990 AGM. He asks you to look through the accounts, saying: 'in view of the increased bank balance, sales and income, I don't expect any questions to be raised! Please let me know if there are any questions you think I might have to face.'

Prepare a note for Albert in reply, based on the accounts below.

Silverbridge Working Men's Club: Balance sheet as at 31 December 1989

	1989		*1988*	
	£	£	£	£
Property		6,000		6,000
Fixtures:				
At beginning of year	28,600		3,900	
Additions	—		40,100	
	28,600		44,000	
Depreciation	10,010		15,400	
At end of year		18,590		28,600
		24,590		34,600
Current assets:				
Stock	7,900		3,520	
Prepayments	720		680	
Bank	8,880		1,200	
	17,500		5,400	
Less: Creditors	10,000		9,000	
		7,500		(3,600)
		32,090		31,000

Accumulated fund:		
B/fwd	31,000	39,200
Surplus of income over expenditure		
(expenditure over income)	1,090	(8,200)
	32,090	31,000

Silverbridge Working Men's Club: Income and expenditure for the year ended 31 December 1989

	1989		1988	
	£	£	£	£
Bar sales		140,000		130,000
Cost of sales		98,000		87,100
Gross profit		42,000		42,900
Other income:				
Interest receivable	—		900	
Gaming machines — net income	14,200		1,300	
Subscriptions	1,100		1,200	
Room hire	500		600	
		15,800		15,700
		57,800		58,600
Wages	37,200		35,000	
Depreciation	10,010		15,400	
Repairs	500		8,000	
Rates, heat & light	9,000		8,400	
		56,710		66,800
Surplus/(deficit)		1,090		(8,200)

Question 23

The Fulke Leisure Group plc is a regional brewer and national hotelier. Accounts for the year to 31 December 19X8 showed:

Balance sheet as at 31 December 19X8:

	19X8		19X7	
	£000	£000	£000	£000
Fixed assets (note 1)		155,960		134,970
Current assets:				
Stock	12,500		12,200	
Debtors	16,700		15,300	
Short-term deposits	48,500		2,000	
Bank	120		125	
	77,820		29,625	

Current liabilities:

Taxation	4,100		3,500	
Trade creditors	11,800		10,000	
Overdrafts	920		4,600	
Dividends	4,400		3,200	
Sundry creditors & accruals	14,780		13,400	
	36,000		34,700	
Net current assets (liabilities)		41,820		(5,075)
		197,780		129,895
Long-term loans		40,000		18,615
		157,780		111,280
Ordinary shares of £1		14,800		12,800
Share premium		65,280		27,280
Retained profits		77,700		71,200
		157,780		111,280

Profit and loss account for the year ended 31 December 19X8:

	19X8	19X7
Turnover	171,700	163,500
Operating costs	150,900	145,900
	20,800	17,600
Income from short-term deposits	1,300	200
	22,100	17,800
Interest payable	2,800	2,300
Profit before tax	19,300	15,500
Taxation	6,500	5,300
Profit after tax	12,800	10,200
Dividends	6,300	4,800
Retained profit for the year	6,500	5,400

Note 1

	Buildings £000	Plant & Fixtures £000	Total £000
Cost:			
b/fwd	100,500	59,500	160,000
Additions	20,000	9,000	29,000
Disposal	(1,200)	(4,500)	(5,700)
c/fwd	119,300	64,000	183,300
Depreciation:			
b/fwd	1,030	24,000	25,030
Charge	330	5,700	6,030
Disposals	(20)	(3,700)	(3,720)
c/fwd	1,340	26,000	27,340

Net book value:

31.12.X8	117,960	38,000	155,960
31.12.X7	99,470	35,500	134,970

Disposals during 19X8 resulted in a gain on property of £500,000 and a loss on plant of £220,000.

Note 2 — Average number of employees:

	19X8	19X7
Breweries	2,500	2,600
Hotels	3,000	2,800
Total	5,500	5,400

You are required to:

(a) Compare the accounts for the two years, using appropriate analytical tools.

(b) Identify any extra information you would find particularly useful in analysing these accounts.

Question 24

You are the audit partner responsible for a client, Land plc, a company whose most recent accounts are shown below. You are due to meet the managing director for lunch. Your audit senior suggests that over lunch you raise the following points:

(a) Distribution costs have gone up by 22%, whereas administration costs have only gone up 20%. This suggests that distribution costs need to be more tightly controlled.

(b) Stock has increased by 23%. Thus tighter stock control seems needed.

(c) Sales per £1 of land and buildings have gone down:

$$\text{1988} \qquad\qquad\qquad \text{1987}$$
$$\frac{1,300}{250} = 5.2 \qquad\qquad \frac{1,000}{120} = 8.3$$

thus a return to the 1988 level of achievement seems desirable.

(d) Gearing, computed as:

$$\frac{\text{Current liabilities + Long-term liabilities}}{\text{Equity + Current liabilities + Long-term liabilities}}$$

is down substantially:

$$\text{1988} \qquad\qquad\qquad\qquad \text{1987}$$
$$\frac{88 + 200}{361 + 88 + 200} = 44\% \qquad\qquad \frac{67 + 200}{210 + 67 + 200} = 56\%$$

Thus the company might reasonably embark on additional borrowing.

Required:

Comment on each of the above points, with reference to the accounts below where appropriate.

Land plc: Profit and loss account for the year ended 31 December 1988

	1988		1987	
	£m	£m	£m	£m
Turnover		1,300		1,000
Cost of sales		936		700
Gross profit		364		300
Distribution costs	208		170	
	72		60	
		280		230
Operating profit		84		70
Interest		20		20
Profit before tax		64		50
Taxation		20		15
Profit after tax		44		35
Dividends — interim	5		5	
proposed	18		12	
		23		17
Retained profit for year		21		18
Retained profit b/fwd		100		82
Retained profit c/fwd		121		100

Land plc: Balance sheet as at 31 December 1988

	1988		1987	
	£m	£m	£m	£m
Fixed assets (note 1)		446		238
Current assets:				
Stock	97		79	
Debtors	96		90	
Bank	10		70	
	203		239	
Current liabilities:				
Creditors	51		40	
Tax	19		15	
Dividend	18		12	
	88		67	
Net current assets		115		172
		561		410
Debentures		200		200
		361		210

	£m	£m
Share capital	70	70
Share premium	40	40
Revaluation reserve	130	—
Retained profit	121	100
	361	210

Note 1: Fixed assets

	Land & buildings £m	Plant £m	Total £m
Cost/value:			
At 1.1.88	120	190	310
Revaluation	130	—	130
Addition	—	110	110
Disposal	—	(10)	(10)
At 31.12.88	250	290	540
Depreciation:			
At 1.1.88	—	72	72
Charge for year	—	30	30
Disposal	—	(8)	(8)
	—	94	94
NBV: 1.1.88	120	118	238
NBV: 31.12.88	250	196	446

Question 25

You are given the following information relating to T plc:

(i)   **The summarized profit and loss accounts for the year ended 31 December:**

	1985 £m	1986 £m
Trading profit	294.7	500.9
Other income	43.3	61.8
Profit before taxation	338.0	562.7
Taxation	151.2	224.1
Profit on ordinary activities after taxation	186.8	338.6
Profit attributable to minority interests	19.1	25.5
Profit before extraordinary items	167.7	313.1
Extraordinary items	11.6	—
Profit for the year	156.1	313.1
Preference dividends	2.0	2.0
	154.1	311.1
Ordinary dividends	45.5	72.8
Retained profit for the year	108.6	238.3

(ii)   **The summarized balance sheets at 31 December:**

	1985	1986
	£m	£m
Fixed assets	791.0	1,577.8
Working capital	810.6	707.6
Total assets *less* current liabilities	1,601.6	2,285.4
Loans repayable after more than one year	427.0	427.0
	1,174.6	1,858.4
Minority interests	60.4	85.9
	1,114.2	1,772.5
Share capital — preference shares of £1 each	20.0	20.0
— ordinary shares of 50 pence each	455.0	525.0
Share premium	81.2	431.2
Retained profits	558.0	796.3
	1,114.2	1,772.5

(iii)   On 1 April 1986, 140 million ordinary shares of 50 pence each were
issued at a price of £3.00 per share to acquire a new subsidiary. The
profits of this new subsidiary were included in the group earnings
from 1 April 1986.

You are required to calculate for T plc, in accordance with the requirements
of Statement of Standard Accounting Practice No 3,

(a)   the earnings per share figures for:
      (i)   the year ended 31 December 1985,
      (ii)   the year ended 31 December 1986;
(b)   The adjusted earnings per share for the year ended 31 December 1986
      to be included as a comparative figure in the 1987 financial statements
      if a 1-for-2 bonus issue were made on 1 August 1987.
                                                                    (CIMA, Stage 3, 1987)

Question 26

The following are the summarized accounts for B Limited, a company with
an accounting year ending on 30 September.

Summarized balance sheets for:

	1985/86		1986/87	
	£000	£000	£000	£000
Tangible fixed assets — at cost *less* depreciation		4,995		12,700
Current assets:				
Stocks	40,145		50,455	
Debtors	40,210		43,370	
Cash at bank	12,092		5,790	
	92,447		99,615	

Creditors: amounts falling due within one year:

Trade creditors	32,604	37,230
Taxation	2,473	3,260
Proposed dividend	1,785	1,985
	36,862	42,475

Net current assets	55,585	57,140
Total assets *less* current liabilities	60,580	69,840

Creditors: amounts falling due after more than one year:

10% Debentures 2006/2010	19,840	19,840
	40,740	50,000

Capital and reserves:

Called-up share capital of £0.25 per share	9,920	9,920
Profit and loss account	30,820	40,080
Shareholders' funds	40,740	50,000

Summarized profit and loss accounts for:

	1985/86 £000	1986/87 £000
Turnover	486,300	583,900
Operating profit	17,238	20,670
Interest payable	1,984	1,984
Profit on ordinary activities before taxation	15,254	18,686
Tax on profit on ordinary activities	5,734	7,026
Profit for the financial year	9,520	11,660
Dividends	2,240	2,400
	7,280	9,260
Retained profit brought forward	23,540	30,820
Retained profit carried forward	30,820	40,080

You are required to:

(a) calculate, for each year, **two** ratios for **each** of the following user groups, which are of particular significance to them:
  (i) shareholders,
  (ii) trade creditors,
  (iii) internal management;
(b) make brief comments upon the changes, between the two years, in the ratios calculated in (a) above.

Question 27

The following accounts for Nailsea Limited for the year ended 30 June 1986 are to be used for all the questions which follow.

Nailsea Limited
Profit and loss account for year ended 30 June 1986

	1986	1985
	£000	£000
Sales	2,280	1,230
Operating costs	(1,618)	(722)
Depreciation	(320)	(270)
Operating profit	342	238
Interest	(27)	—
Profit before tax	315	238
Tax	(140)	(110)
Profit after tax	175	128
Extraordinary items (note 1)	(75)	—
Profit after tax and extraordinary items	100	128
Dividend	(85)	(80)
Retained profit for year	15	48

Balance sheet as at 30 June 1986

	1986		1985	
	£000	£000	£000	£000
Fixed assets (note 2)		2,640		2,310
Current assets:				
Stock	450		275	
Debtors	250		100	
Bank	78		23	
	778		398	
Less: Creditors due within one year:				
Creditors	190		130	
Taxation	140		110	
Dividend	85		80	
	415		320	
Net current assets		363		78
		3,003		2,388
Less: Creditors falling due after more than 1 year:				
9% Debentures (2006)		300		—
		2,703		2,338
Share capital (fully paid £1 shares)		1,600		1,400
Share premium account		300		200
Retained profits		803		788
		2,703		2,388

Note 1
The extraordinary item represents redundancy payments and other closure costs.

Note 2: *Schedule of fixed assets:*

	Land & buildings *£000*	*Plant & machinery* *£000*	*Total* *£000*
Cost:			
At 1 July 1985	1,500	1,350	2,850
Additions	400	250	650
At 30 June 1986	1,900	1,600	3,500
Depreciation:			
At 1 July 1985	—	540	540
Charge for year at 20%	—	320	320
At 30 June 1986	—	860	860
Net book value at 30 June 1986	1,900	740	2,640

1. **You are required** to prepare a statement of source and application of funds for Nailsea Limited for the year ended 30 June 1986.

2. **You are required** to prepare the following ratios for Nailsea Limited:
    (a) return on capital employed;
    (b) net profit margin;
    (c) sales turnover ratio;
    (d) current ratio;
    (e) liquid ratio;
    (f) stock turnover ratio;
    (g) days debtors;
    (h) debt: equity ratio;
    (i) earnings per share;
    (j) dividend per share.

    Note: Calculate for 1986 and 1985 using closing year asset values.

3. **You are required** to comment on the performance of Nailsea Limited, incorporating the information you have prepared in Questions 1 and 2, from the viewpoint of:
    (a) the company management;
    (b) the shareholders.
                                                                  (Cert. Dip. F. A. 1986)

Question 28

The abbreviated accounts for Backwell Limited are given below. Backwell is a private manufacturing firm operating wholly within the UK.

Backwell Limited
Profit and loss accounts for the years ending 31 December

	1986		*1985*		*1984*	
	£000	*£000*	*£000*	*£000*	*£000*	*£000*
Sales		660		620		600
Cost of sales		(330)		(300)		(300)
Gross profit		330		320		300

Operating expenses	60		100		85	
Depreciation	105		65		65	
Interest	20		—		—	
	—	(185)	—	(165)	—	(150)
Net profit before tax and dividend		145		155		150
Tax		(50)		(50)		(50)
Net profit after tax		95		105		100
Dividend proposed		(45)		(40)		(40)
Profit retained for year		50		65		60

Balance sheets as at 31 December

	1986		1985		1984	
	£000	£000	£000	£000	£000	£000
Fixed assets: Cost		1,050		650		650
Depreciation		(460)		(355)		(290)
		590		295		360
Current assets:						
Stocks: Raw materials	60		55		50	
Finished goods and work						
in progress	140		80		40	
Debtors	160		120		80	
Cash	130		155		100	
	490		410		270	
Less: Creditors due within one Year:						
trade creditors	90		70		60	
Tax	50		50		50	
Dividend	45		40		40	
	185		160		150	
Net current assets		305		250		120
Less: Creditors due after more than one year:						
Loan stock		(200)		—		—
		695		545		480
Capital and reserves:						
Ordinary shares of £1 fully paid		350		300		300
Share premium		50		—		—
Retained profits		295		245		180
		695		545		480

Required:

(a) Prepare a statement of source and application of funds for the years
ended 31 December 1986 and 31 December 1985.

(b) Using the above statements and any ratios you consider helpful,
comment on the performance of Backwell Limited from the viewpoint
of:

(i)   a small shareholder in the company;
(ii) a small company about to supply goods and become a creditor of Backwell Limited.

(Cert. Dip. F. A. 1986)

Question 29

Below are the balance sheets and profit and loss accounts of two companies in the brewing industry:

Balance sheets as at 31 December 1988:

	G plc		H plc	
	£000	£000	£000	£000
Fixed assets — tangible		472,000		14,300
Current assets:				
Stock	36,000		700	
Trade debtors	25,000		410	
Prepayments etc.	11,000		2,530	
Cash	5,000		6,940	
	77,000		10,580	
Current liabilities:				
Trade creditors	39,800		600	
Dividends	3,900		450	
Tax	7,300		1,200	
Sundry accruals etc.	38,000		560	
Current instalments on debentures	50,400		—	
Overdraft	5,500		—	
	144,900		2,810	
Net current assets/(liabilities)		(67,900)		7,770
		404,100		22,070
Debentures		68,000		—
		336,100		22,070
Share capital		67,800		750
Reserves		268,300		21,320
		336,100		22,070

Profit and loss accounts for the year ended 31 December 1988:

	G plc		H plc	
	£000	£000	£000	£000
Turnover		387,400		11,500
Cost of sales		204,400		6,100
		183,000		5,400
Distribution	12,200		1,930	
Administration	136,400		1,270	

		148,600		3,200
Operating profit		34,400		2,200
Interest receivable	1,100		770	
Interest payable	(13,700)		—	
		(13,590)		770
Profit before tax		20,810		2,970
Tax		7,500		1,200
		13,310		1,770
Dividends		6,500		600
Retained profit		6,810		1,170

Required:
Using appropriate ratios, compare the two companies.

Question 30

The following are the summarized accounts of two trading companies, each of which has recently approached your bank requesting a loan of £150,000 to acquire the shares of a director who is about to retire.

Revenue accounts for 1985

	Easthope Ltd		*Quilter Ltd*	
	£000	*£000*	*£000*	*£000*
Turnover		2,050		2,620
Less: Cost of sales		1,435		1,890
Gross profit		615		730
Less: Depreciation	50		120	
Other indirect expenses	445	495	480	600
Net profit		120		130

Balance sheet at 31 December 1985

	£000	*£000*
Ordinary share capital	500	600
Retained profit	100	300
	600	900
Current liabilities	260	300
	860	1,200
Premises	50	430
Other fixed assets	355	245
Current assets	455	525
	860	1,200

You discover that neither company needs to replace fixed assets in the near future. The 1985 results are expected to be repeated for the next few years, and the directors plan to pay out the entire profits in the form of dividends.

Required:
(a) The following calculations, ratios and percentages presented in a tabular format for each company:
    (i)   Funds generated from operations.
    (ii)   Proprietorship ratio.
    (iii) Working capital ratio.
    (iv) Net profit as a percentage of sales.
    (v)   Return on year-end balance of shareholders' equity.
(b) Based on your findings under (a), state the areas in which Easthope appears to be stronger and the areas in which Quilter appears to be stronger.
(c) To which company would you be more willing to grant loan facilities? Give your reasons.

(AIB, 1986)

Question 31

Summarized below are the accounts of two companies in the food processing and distribution industry.

Balance sheets as at 31 December 19X8:

	Skin plc		Bone plc	
	£m	£m	£m	£m
Fixed assets		271		65
Current assets:				
Stock	46		110	
Debtors	124		70	
Cash	15		10	
	185		190	
Current liabilities	154		170	
Net current assets		31		20
		302		85
Long-term liabilities		25		10
		277		75
Share capital		200		50
Retained profits		77		25
		277		75

Profit and loss accounts for the year ended 31 December 19X8:

	Skin plc		Bone plc	
	£m	£m	£m	£m
Sales		1,020		1,500
Cost of sales		775		1,380
Gross profit		245		120
Distribution	120		40	
Administration	50		60	

	170	100
Operating profits	75	20
Interest	2	2
Profit before tax	73	18
Tax	23	7
Profit available to shareholders	50	11
Dividends	22	8
Retained profit for year	28	3

Required:
Compare the two companies.

Question 32

The summarized accounts of Gee Whiz Electronics Ltd for the last two years are shown below. The company is a wholesaler in the electrical trade.

Profit and loss accounts

	1986	1987
	£	£
Sales	2,154,203	3,196,124
Less: Cost of sales	1,421,774	2,301,209
Gross profit	732,429	894,915
Less: Expenses	581,635	627,819
Net profit	150,794	267,096
Less: Taxation	52,778	93,484
Retained profit for year	98,016	173,612
Retained profit brought forward	151,079	249,095
Retained profit carried forward	249,095	422,707

Balance sheets

	31 December 1986		31 December 1987	
	£	£	£	£
Fixed assets		174,917		368,512
Current assets:				
Stock	125,217		148,217	
Debtors	317,412		352,140	
Cash	109,120		99,146	
	551,749		599,503	
Less: Creditors	77,571	474,178	145,308	454,195
		649,095		822,707
Share capital		400,000		400,000
Retained profits		249,095		422,707
		649,095		822,707

Required:

Comment upon the changes you can see between the 1986 and 1987 results, calculating and using at least **FIVE** accounting ratios in your review.

(CIB, 1988)

Question 33

Nibthrow plc: Balance sheet as at 31 December 19X7:

	19X7		19X6	
	£000	£000	£000	£000
Fixed assets (note 1)		27,600		13,200
Current assets:				
Stock	25,000		17,000	
Debtors	13,700		11,500	
Bank	4,800		3,000	
	43,500		31,500	
Current liabilities:				
Trade creditors	21,650		14,980	
Taxation	1,770		570	
Dividends	780		460	
Overdrafts	9,000		490	
Sundry creditors & accruals	7,000		5,500	
	40,200		22,000	
Net current assets		3,300		9,500
		30,900		22,700
Long-term loans		2,400		2,100
		28,500		20,600
Ordinary shares of £1		9,800		8,300
Share premium		12,940		10,600
Retained profit		5,760		1,700
		28,500		20,600

Nibthrow plc: Profit and loss account for the year ended 31 December 19X7:

	19X7		19X6	
	£000	£000	£000	£000
Turnover		90,000		63,200
Cost of sales		53,200		38,700
		36,800		24,500

Distribution costs	21,140	14,530
Administration costs	7,390	4,470
	28,530	19,000
Operating profit	8,270	5,500
Interest payable	1,800	700
Profit before tax	6,470	4,800
Taxation	1,410	570
Profit attributable to shareholders	5,060	4,230
Dividends	1,000	600
Retained profit	4,060	3,630

Note 1:

	Land & building £000	Plant & fixtures £000	Total £000
Fixed assets:			
Cost:			
At 1.1.X7	9,000	7,000	16,000
Additions	10,600	6,500	17,100
Disposals	(800)	(900)	(1,700)
At 31.12.X7	18,800	12,600	31,400
Depreciation:			
At 1.1.X7	—	2,800	2,800
Charge for year	—	1,500	1,500
Disposals	—	(500)	(500)
At 31.12.X7	—	3,800	3,800
Written down value:			
At 31.12.X7	18,800	8,800	27,600
At 1.1.X7	9,000	4,200	13,200

Profit on sale of fixed assets was £170,000

Required:
Using appropriate analytical techniques, report on how the company developed during 19X7.

Question 34

The latest balance sheet and profit and loss account summary of Sunlight Ltd, a manufacturing company, is as follows:

Sunlight Ltd: Balance sheet as at 31 March 1979

	£	£		£	£
Authorized share capital —			*Fixed assets:*		
400,000 £1 ordinary shares		400,000	Freehold property (book		
Issued and fully paid — 200,000			value		240,000
£1 ordinary shares		200,000	Plant and machinery (cost,		
Capital reserves		100,000	Less: Depreciation)		400,000
Revenue reserves		400,000	Motor vehicles (cost,		
Shareholders' funds employed:		700,000	Less: Depreciation)		100,000
			Office furniture (cost,		
			Less: Depreciation		100,000
					840,000
Loan capital					
200,000 10% £1 debentures					
(secured on freehold property					
— repayable 1991)		200,000	*Current assets:*		
Book value of long-term funds		900,000	Stocks	500,000	
Current liabilities:	£		Debtors	200,000	
Trade creditors	119,200		Investments	60,000	760,000
Bank overdraft					
(secured)	439,200				
Current taxation	88,000				
Dividend payable	53,600	700,000			
		£1,600,000			£1,600,000

Summary profit and loss account for the year ended 31 March 1979

	£
Sales (all on credit)	2,000,000
Profit after charging all expenses except debenture interest	220,000
Less: Debenture interest (gross)	20,000
Profit before taxation	200,000
Less: Corporation tax on the taxable profit for the year	88,000
Profit after taxation	112,000
Less: Ordinary dividend proposed	53,600
Retained profit transferred to revenue reserve	£58,400

Notes:
Purchases for the year were £1,080,000.
Cost of sales for the year was £1,500,000.
The market price of a Sunlight Ltd ordinary share as at 31 March 1979 was £4.00.
Income tax is to be taken at 33%. ACT is ignored.
The managing director has suggested that a figure representing the company's goodwill be computed and included in the balance sheet under that heading with the shareholders' funds increased by its value. The company estimates the current value of its freehold property at £440,000.

You are required:

(a)   To compute the following ratios:

(i)   primary ratio (using the *book* value of total assets as capital employed);
(ii)   secondary ratio — the profit margin;
(iii)   secondary ratio — the turnover of capital;
(iv)   current ratio;
(v)   liquid ratio;
(vi)   debtors' ratio;
(vii)   proprietary ratio;
(viii) stock turnover ratio;
(ix)   dividend yield;
(x)   price earnings ratio and its reciprocal.

(b) To write a brief comment on the *liquidity* of Sunlight Ltd, stating the reference points to which relevant ratios can be compared.

(c) To write a memorandum to the managing director explaining the nature of goodwill from an accountant's point of view, and stating, *with reasons*, whether or not you recommend the inclusion of a figure for goodwill in the balance sheet.

(ACA, P3, December 1979)

Question 35

The financial information provided below is for two companies that operate in similar retail fields, using the same business and accounting policies.

Balance sheets at 30.6.82

	Cab Ltd (£000)	Horse Ltd (£000)
Ordinary shares	350	470
Capital reserves	65	35
Revenue reserves	185	287
10% debentures	50	60
Current liabilities:		
Bank overdraft	26	24
Trade creditors	97	132
Other current liabilities and provisions	42	48
	815	1,056
Fixed assets (at book values):		
Land and buildings	286	381
Plant and equipment	218	342
Motor vehicles	59	62
Current assets:		
Stock	122	97
Trade debtors	124	166
Cash	6	8
	815	1,056

Profit and loss accounts for year ended 30 June 1982

	Cab Ltd (£000)	Cab Ltd (£000)	Horse Ltd (£000)	Horse Ltd (£000)
Sales		747		570
Cost of sales:				
Opening stock	102		92	
Purchases	588		381	
	690		473	
Closing stock	122		96	
		568		377
Gross profit		179		193
Operating expenses				
Selling and distribution	64		60	
Administration and management	31		29	
Interest — Debentures	5		6	
— Other	4		2	
		104		97
Net profit		75		96
Provision for taxation		37		45
		38		51
Provision for dividend		24		37
Transfer to revenue reserve		14		14

You have received a request from a client to prepare a report on the two companies Cab and Horse. Specifically your client requires a comparative analysis of the efficiency of operations and the short-term financial strength of the two firms.

You are required to:

(i)   Calculate for each company at least six ratios which you consider most appropriate for indicating the efficiency of operations and short-term financial strength of the two firms.

(ii)   Using the financial information provided above and the ratios you have calculated, prepare a report which analyses and compares the efficiency of operations and short-term financial strength of the Cab and Horse Companies.

Question 36

Your friend Dr Wortle owns a small number of ordinary shares in two companies, Barrow Ltd and Quorn Ltd, both of which are in the retail clothing trade. Observing that the earnings per share figure for Quorn Ltd is higher than that of Barrow Ltd he has come to the conclusion that the management of Barrow Ltd could usefully learn from the management policies of Quorn Ltd and proposes to raise this matter at the AGM of Barrow Ltd. Dr Wortle has extracted information from the accounts of the two companies which he has sent to you, and he proposes to visit your office in order to discuss the performance of the two companies.

You are required to prepare notes of points to be made to Dr Wortle at this meeting with reference to the accounts presented below.

Profit and loss account for the year ended 31 March 1881

	Barrow Ltd		Quorn Ltd	
	£000	£000	£000	£000
Turnover		10,600		4,800
Operating profit		816		355
Less:				
Debenture interest	24		81	
Short-term interest	14		36	
		38		117
Profit before taxation		778		238
Taxation		36		24
Profit after taxation		742		214
Dividends		214		140
Retained profit for the year		528		74
Retained profit b/fwd		2302		1031
Retained profit c/fwd		2830		1105
Earnings per share		46.4p		66.9p

Balance sheet as at 31 March 1981

	Barrow Ltd		Quorn Ltd	
	£000	£000	£000	£000
Fixed assets		4,620		2,400
Current assets:				
Stock	810		1,150	
Debtors	170		240	
Cash	200		10	
	1,180		1,400	
Less current liabilities:				
Creditors	700		720	
Overdraft	90		240	
Taxation	120		70	
Dividends	160		115	
	1,070		1,145	
Net current assets		110		255
		4,730		2,655
Share capital:				
Ordinary shares of £1		1,600		320
Share premium account				150
Revenue reserves		2,830		1,105
		4,430		1,575

8% debenture stock	300	—
7½% debenture stock	—	1,080
Deferred taxation	—	—
	4,730	2,655
Current ordinary share price	£3.50	£3.35

Question 37

Splint Ltd and Bandage Ltd are two companies in the medical supply industry; extracts from the accounts of the two companies are presented below. You are required to prepare a selection of accounting ratios relevant to the problem of comparing the profitability, solvency and financial structure of the two companies and to summarize your conclusions.

Balance sheet as at 31 December 1982

	Splint Ltd		Bandage Ltd	
	£000	£000	£000	£000
Ordinary shares of £1		2,000		2,280
Retained profits		3,000		4,020
		5,000		6,300
Debentures — repayable 1990		1,285		480
		6,285		6,780
Fixed assets		5,000		4,500
Less: Depreciation		1,000		1,560
		4,000		2,940
Current assets:				
Stock	2,000		3,180	
Debtors	990		1,320	
Cash and short-term deposits	1,580		1,560	
	4,570		6,060	
Current liabilities:				
Bank loan	900		900	
Creditors	1,385		1,320	
	2,285		2,220	
Net current assets		2,285		3,840
		6,285		6,780

Profit and loss account for the year ended 31 December 1982

	Splint Ltd		Bandage Ltd	
	£000	£000	£000	£000
Sales		24,000		14,000
Cost of sales		20,000		11,300
Gross profit		4,000		2,700
Operating expenses	2,050		1,470	
Depreciation	270		240	

Long-term interest	130		24	
Short-term interest	110	2,560	66	1,800
Net profit before taxation		1,440		900
Taxation		720		450
Net profit after taxation		720		450

Question 38

Elusive Engineering Public Limited Company has just joined the Midland Light Engineering Trade Association's Interfirm Comparison scheme. Exhibit III depicts the ratios for the company (Firm D) and four of its local competitors.

The ratios are issued to each participating company with a brief report commenting upon the company's performance, apparent strengths and weaknesses when compared with its competitors.

You are required to prepare the brief report, commenting on the company's performance.

Exhibit III
Midland Light Engineering Trade Association

Ratios			*Firms*		
Overall	A	B	C	D	E
1. Operating profit/operating assets (%)	24.4	20.3	19.1	18.7	14.2
2. Operating profit/sales (%)	17.9	13.8	8.3	12.4	8.9
3. Sales/operating assets (times)	1.36	1.47	2.3	1.51	1.6
Departmental costs (as a % of sales)					
4. Production costs	72.1	77.2	76.4	78.8	77.5
5. Distribution and marketing costs	5.7	5.1	11.1	6.0	8.7
6. Administration costs	4.3	3.9	4.2	2.8	4.9
Production costs (as a % of sales)					
7. Material costs	31.1	34.2	31.4	32.7	34.3
8. Works labour costs	17.9	23.0	16.8	27.0	28.5
9. Production overheads	23.4	20.0	28.2	19.1	14.7
Asset utilization (£'s per £1,000 of sales)					
3a. Operating assets	735	680	435	662	625
10. Current assets	334	253	141	341	242
11. Fixed assets	401	427	294	321	383
Current asset utilization (£'s per £1,000 of sales)					
12. Materials stock	34	70	32	60	43
13. Work-in-progress	53	84	17	63	90
14. Finished stock	62	32	19	88	44
15. Debtors	185	67	73	130	65
Fixed asset utilization (£'s per £1,000 of sales)					
16. Land and buildings	210	221	75	130	230
17. Plant and machinery	271	182	143	157	93
18. Vehicles	20	24	76	34	60

(Cert. Dip. F.A., 1981)

Suggested solutions to questions 1–32

Question 1: solution

(i) Ratio analysis is a tool used in the interpretation of financial accounts, whereby the relationship between amounts is expressed as a proportion or percentage.

(ii) Ratios can be compared with external or internal data. External data will be drawn from the accounts of competing businesses with whom a meaningful comparison can be made, and will normally relate to companies in the same industry, although the definition of industrial classification may pose practical problems. Comparison may be made with industrial average figures published by governments or private organizations, with individual competing businesses, or with data generated by an interfirm comparative study.

Internal data for comparison will include the accounts of previous years, budgeted target ratios, and the accounts of other divisions within the same organization.

(iii) Problems in producing ratios arise because:

(a) There are inherent deficiencies in financial accounts as a basis for decision-making. In times of inflation the historical cost accounts tend to understate the economic value represented by expenses shown in the profit and loss account and assets recorded in the balance sheet. Differences in the accounting policies chosen and the ways in which estimates are made may render the accounts of different companies uncomparable.

(b) There is a lack of comparability between the balance sheets of different companies made up to different accounting dates, particularly in the case of companies operating in an industry subject to seasonal fluctuations in their trading pattern.

(c) Published accounts only contain a limited amount of data, particularly in the case of small limited companies. Therefore the data required for detailed analysis may not be available.

(d) Published accounts may be produced so long after the accounting year end as to be of little value.

(e) The reporting entity may not be the entity with which the user is concerned. For example, an employee may be interested in assessing the future prospects of the business unit by which they are employed, while only the accounts of the employing company are available, embracing a number of business units.

(f) There is no authoritative definition of the terms used in ratio analysis, so that there is a danger that terms will be mis-understood.

(g) There is a danger, when using accounting ratios, that the significance of individual items in absolute terms will be forgotten.

(iv) (a) One example of a liquidity ratio is the 'acid test' normally computed as:

$$\frac{\text{Current assets} - \text{Stock}}{\text{Current liabilities}}$$

The objective of this ratio is to express the relationship between assets and liabilities that will be received or paid in the short term, and some authorities argue that other items apart from stock which are not liquid in the short term should be excluded from the computation of this ratio.

(b) One example of a profitability ratio is the return on long-term funds employed, normally expressed as:

$$\frac{\text{Profit before tax} + \text{Long-term interest}}{\text{Share capital} + \text{Reserves} + \text{Long-term liabilities}}$$

This is a form of return on capital employed ratio.

(c) The ratio of earnings per share is an investment ratio. It is computed as:

$$\frac{\text{Profit after tax, minority interest and preference dividends,}}{\text{Number of ordinary shares in issue and ranking for dividend}}$$

Question 2: solution

(a) The equity yield ratio expresses the relationship between the amount of the dividend paid relating to each ordinary share and the share price, being computed as:

$$\frac{\text{Dividend per share}}{\text{Share price}}$$

This tells the shareholder the return earned in the form of dividend as a percentage of the *current* share price.

(b) The price–earnings ratio expresses the relationship between the current share price and the earnings per share, being computed as:

$$\frac{\text{Share price}}{\text{Earnings per share}}$$

This ratio gives us an indication of how highly the market values the earnings of the company, a high P/E ratio indicating optimism and a low P/E ratio indicating pessimism.

(c) The dividend cover ratio expresses the relationship between profit available for distribution to ordinary shareholders and the amount of the dividend, being computed as:

$$\frac{\text{Earnings per share}}{\text{Dividend per share}}$$

The higher the ratio, the better the chance of maintaining — and perhaps increasing — the dividend.

Question 3: solution

(a) **Return on equity — 1982:**

$$
\begin{array}{cc}
\textit{Riverside} & \textit{Orlando} \\
\dfrac{600 - (500 \times 15\%)}{2,000 + 1,500} = 15\% & \dfrac{900 - (4,000 \times 15\%)}{1,000 + 1,000} = 15\%
\end{array}
$$

(b) **Capital structure:** Riverside has obtained 12.5% of its long-term finance from borrowing, while the figure for Orlando is 67%. Thus Orlando is highly geared while Riverside is lower geared. The effect of gearing is that when there is a fluctuation in the operating profit of a company, because the claims of the suppliers of fixed-interest finance are fixed in monetary terms, the impact of the fluctuation on the profit available to ordinary shareholders in magnified. This effect can be measured by a ratio known as the degree of capital gearing. For Orlando any fluctuation in operating profit will lead to a fluctuation in profit available to shareholders 1.14 times greater; for Riverside the equivalent figure is three times. This is illustrated by the computation of the prospective return on equity in the event of a fluctuation of 50% from the 1982 operating profit level.

For ordinary shareholders the effect of higher gearing is to increase their risk, since the effect of any fluctuation in profit on their income is magnified. The return on equity of Riverside will be subject to far less fluctuation than that of Orlando. For management there is a problem with high gearing, in that the cash outflow involved in paying interest charges is required even in years of low profit; for Orlando, in the event of a fall in operating profit of 50%, there will actually be a loss attributable to shareholders for the year. Moreover, a highly geared company is likely to have difficulty in raising further borrowings, so that in the event of cashflow problems Riverside will have more room for manoeuvre than Orlando. In view of the cyclical nature of the industry, the management of Orlando would be well advised to retain a high proportion of profits in the business in good years in order to build up the resources to cover cash outflows in bad years.

Fluctuations in return on equity:
Minimum profit before interest is:

$$\text{For Riverside } 600 \times 50\% = 300$$
$$\text{For Orlando } 900 \times 50\% = 450$$

Maximum profit before interest is:

$$\text{For Riverside } 600 \times 150\% = 900$$
$$\text{For Orlando } 900 \times 150\% = 1{,}350$$

Maximum and minimum returns on equity can therefore be computed as follows:

	Riverside	*Orlando*
Minimum	$\dfrac{300 - (500 \times 15\%)}{2{,}000 + 1{,}500}$	$\dfrac{450 - (4{,}000 \times 15\%)}{1{,}000 + 1{,}000}$
	$= 6.4\%$	$= (7.5)\%$
Maximum	$\dfrac{900 - (500 \times 15\%)}{2{,}000 + 1{,}500}$	$\dfrac{1{,}350 - (4{,}000 \times 15\%)}{1{,}000 + 1{,}000}$
	$= 23.6\%$	$= 37.5\%$

Workings:
Ratios computed to illustrate the answer:

	Riverside	*Orlando*
Gearing	$\dfrac{500}{4{,}000} = 12.5\%$	$\dfrac{4{,}000}{6{,}000} = 67\%$
Degree of capital gearing	$\dfrac{600}{525} = 1.14$	$\dfrac{900}{300} = 3$

Tutorial note:
This question could have been answered solely by reference to the ratios specifically required by the examiner. However, the computation of additional ratios helped to produce a fuller answer.

Question 4: solution

(a) Summary profit and loss accounts:

	A Ltd		B Ltd	
	Year 1	*Year 2*	*Year 1*	*Year 2*
	£000	*£000*	*£000*	*£000*
Trading profit	110	190	110	190
Finance charges	30	30	75	75
Profit before tax	80	160	35	115
Tax	40	80	17.5	57.5
Dividend	40	80	17.5	57.5

(b) After-tax profit as a percentage of ordinary share capital:

	A Ltd	B Ltd
Year 1	$\dfrac{40}{800} = 5\%$	$\dfrac{17.5}{500} = 3.5\%$

$$\text{Year 2} \qquad \frac{80}{800} = 10\% \qquad \frac{17.5}{500} = 11.5\%$$

(c) **Discussion of returns:** Each of these companies has earned the same return on total funds employed in year 1 and has enjoyed the same increase in return on total funds in year 2. However, in year 1 A Ltd earned a rate of return on equity of 5% while B Ltd only achieved a rate of 3.5%. In Year 2 the relative position is changed with A Ltd achieving a return of 10% and B Ltd achieving a return on equity of 11.5%.

The reason for this is the effect of 'gearing'. A Ltd derives only 20% of its total resources from borrowing, whereas B Ltd derives 50% of its resources from borrowing. The higher a company's borrowings, the higher it is said to be 'geared'. Because lenders have an entitlement to interest of a fixed amount, irrespective of the level of profits, then in the event of any fluctuation in trading profits the proprietors of the business, who are entitled to the residue of profit after interest has been paid, will find that residue of profit fluctuates by a greater proportion than the fluctuation in trading profit. This effect can be measured by a ratio known as the degree of capital gearing, computed as:

$$\frac{\text{Profit before interest}}{\text{Profit after interest}}$$

The proportion by which the trading profit fluctuates, multiplied by the degree of capital gearing, gives us the proportion by which profit attributable to the proprietors will fluctuate. In year 1 the degree of capital gearing for each company is:

$$\text{A Ltd} \quad \frac{100}{80} = 1.375 \qquad\qquad \text{B Ltd} \quad \frac{110}{35} = 3.14$$

Thus B Ltd is subject to more violent fluctuations in the return on equity than A Ltd because of higher gearing.

Question 5: solution

Forest Ltd and Beechwood Ltd

While both these companies have a similar return on capital employed, an examination of the secondary ratios shows a substantial difference between the operations of the two companies. Beechwood Ltd achieves a higher profit on sales, while Forest Ltd achieves higher sales in relation to the assets it employs. In order to explain these differences it would be useful to have a detailed breakdown of gross assets, in order to analyse asset turnover, and a detailed profit and loss account, in order to explain the net profit percentages.

Both companies have the same rate of return on total funds employed and on long-term funds employed, but Beechwood Ltd achieves a very much higher rate of return on shareholders' funds. We would expect such a difference to be explained by differences in gearing, and if we look at long-term loans as a proportion of long-term funds employed, Beechwood Ltd is clearly far more highly geared. High gearing does, of course, carry attendant risks and this is demonstrated by the fact that Forest Ltd has a very much higher interest cover ratio.

Ratios — as required by question:

		Forest Ltd	*Beechwood Ltd*
(i)	Profit percentage	$\dfrac{400}{7,400} = 5.4\%$	$\dfrac{600}{7,000} = 8.6\%$
(ii)	Asset turnover	$\dfrac{7,400}{2,400} = 3.1\%$	$\dfrac{7,000}{3,600} = 1.9\%$
(iii)	Percentage return on capital employed	$\dfrac{400}{2,400} = 16\frac{2}{3}\%$	$\dfrac{600}{3,600} = 16\frac{2}{3}\%$
(iv)	Percentage return on long-term funds	$\dfrac{400}{2,000} = 20\%$	$\dfrac{600}{3,000} = 20\%$
(v)	Percentage return on shareholders' equity	$\dfrac{340}{1,500} = 22.7\%$	$\dfrac{360}{1,000} = 36\%$

Additional ratios — to illustrate answer:

	Forest Ltd	*Beechwood Ltd*
Long-term borrowings as a percentage of long-term funds	$\dfrac{500}{2,000} = 25\%$	$\dfrac{2,000}{3,000} = 66\frac{2}{3}\%$
Interest cover	$\dfrac{400}{60} = 6.7$	$\dfrac{600}{240} = 2\frac{1}{2}$

Tutorial note:

The points raised by this question are very straightforward. By giving the two companies identical ROCE ratios based on total funds employed and on long-term funds employed, the examiner has focused our attention very clearly on the contrast in the secondary ratios and the difference in return on shareholders' funds.

Note that to illustrate the answer it is reasonable to compute additional ratios. While the question is set in a form that directs the student's attention to profitability ratios, the link with the gearing ratios is something that is left to the student to identify.

Question 6: solution

Aix Limited

(a) Ratios — as required by question:

	1978	*1979*
Liquid ratio	$\dfrac{120}{10 + 110} = 1$	$\dfrac{160 + 30}{40 + 120} = 1.2$
Average rate of stock turnover	$\dfrac{480}{120} = 4$	$\dfrac{660}{150} = 4.4$

Net profit as a percentage of sales	$\dfrac{60}{800} = 7.5\%$	$\dfrac{78}{1100} = 7.1\%$
Earnings as a percentage of long-term capital employed	$\dfrac{60}{270} = 22.2\%$	$\dfrac{102}{539} = 18.9\%$
Net earnings for ordinary shareholders as a percentage of equity	$\dfrac{60}{270} = 22.2\%$	$\dfrac{78}{339} = 23\%$
Ratio of sales to long-term capital employed	$\dfrac{800}{270} = 3$	$\dfrac{1{,}100}{539} = 2$

Note — computation of long-term funds:

	1978	1979
Average equity	$\dfrac{240 + 300}{2} = 270$	$\dfrac{300 + 378}{2} = 339$
Average long-term loan	Nil	200
Average long-term funds	270	539

(b) The substantial improvement in the liquid ratio would be even greater if it were not for the proposed dividend in 1979. The increase in the stock turnover ratio suggests that management has tightened its control on working capital during the year, but the major factor has been the raising of £200,000 of debentures, making possible repayment of the overdraft.

Net profit as a percentage of sales has fallen slightly, but this is after deduction of debenture interest in 1979. If we add back debenture interest then earnings as a percentage of sales would remain at 7.5% in 1978 and in 1979 would be 102/1,100 = 9.3%, a marked improvement.

By contrast, the asset turnover ratio has dropped from 3 to 2, so that the net effect of higher profit margins and a reduction in the level of activity generated from assets is a moderate reduction in the return in long-term funds employed (from 22.2% to 18.9%). Despite this drop, return on shareholders' funds has increased slightly owing to the increase in grearing following the issue of debentures.

A funds statement would be useful in looking at this company, and in particular would highlight the very substantial new investment in fixed assets. This investment has not yet generated a corresponding increase in turnover — hence the lower asset turnover ratio. If, in the future, turnover can be expected to rise as the new fixed assets become more fully utilized, then the company can expect higher profitability but also an increased demand for working capital.

Tutorial note:
The required ratios are defined with commendable precision. Note that since proposed dividend is not paid until after the year end, average equity is calculated by reference to a year end figure of retained profit with the proposed dividend added back. Note also that loan interest has to be computed — it is not given directly in the question.

Question 7: solution

(a)   Maximon Ltd — statement of source and application of funds for the year ended 30 June 1982:

	£	£
Source of funds:		
Profit before tax		146,000
Adjustments for items not involving movement of funds:		
Depreciation		61,600
Loss on sale of fixed asset		9,600
Total generated from operations		217,200
Funds from other sources:		
Sale of fixed assets	17,900	
Issue of shares for cash	50,000	
Issue of debentures	200,000	
		267,900
		485,100
Application of funds:		
Purchase of fixed assets	195,400	
Tax paid	63,800	
Dividend paid	60,000	
		319,200
		165,900
Increase/decrease in working capital:		
Increase in stock	29,900	
Increase in debtors	60,600	
(increase in creditors)	(4,900)	
	85,600	
Movement in net liquid funds:		
Increase in bank balance	80,300	
		165,900

(b)   Accounting ratios:

	1981	1982
Current ratio	$\dfrac{366,000}{291,600} = 1.3$	$\dfrac{465,800}{228,700} = 2$
Acid test	$\dfrac{135,800}{291,600} = 0.5$	$\dfrac{196,400 + 9,300}{228,700} = 0.9$
Gearing (based on total funds)	$\dfrac{291,600}{520,000 + 291,600} = 36\%$	$\dfrac{228,700 + 200,000}{789,000 + 228,700} = 42\%$
Return on equity (pre-tax)	$\dfrac{151,300}{520,000} = 29.1\%$	$\dfrac{146,000}{589,000} = 24.8\%$
Return on long-term funds	$\dfrac{151,300}{520,000} = 29.1\%$	$\dfrac{176,000}{789,000} = 22.3\%$
Return on total funds	$\dfrac{160,500}{520,000 + 291,600} = 19.8\%$	$\dfrac{176,000}{789,000 + 228,700} = 17.3\%$

In 1981 both the current ratio and the acid test indicated serious liquidity problems; these ratios improved substantially in 1982. From the funds statement we can see that the company has substantially increased working capital during the year, paying off the overdraft and substantially increasing stock and debtors.

The company has also invested heavily in new fixed assets. To finance the investment in fixed assets and additional working capital retained profits alone have, understandably, not been sufficient. Accordingly, the company has raised £50,000 from a rights issue and £200,000 from an issue of debentures. Although there was previously no long-term borrowing the effect is only a modest increase in total gearing, because of the repayment of the overdraft.

Because of the move during the year from short-term to long-term borrowing, comparison of the figures for return on long-term funds may be rather misleading. There has been some drop in the return on total funds, and a rather larger drop in the return on equity; the difference reflects the higher cost of the debenture interest compared to bank overdraft interest. The drop in return on total funds is interesting, and it would be helpful to know the turnover figure so as to be able to compute the secondary ratios. One suspects that, as a result of the easing of pressure on liquidity following the debenture issue, the company may have relaxed its control over debtors and stock thus tieing up its resources unprofitably.

To summarize, a liquidity crisis has been averted thanks to the raising of a long-term loan, with a consequent increase in gearing and in finance costs.

There has also been some drop in profitability that warrants further investigation.

Tutorial note:

An interesting question, which links funds flow analysis and ratio analysis. Note how the two approaches complement each other, and together give us a fuller picture.

Question 8: solution

Report to the directors of Unigear Ltd

In accordance with your instructions we report on the results of your company for the year to 31 December 1972. Our views are based in part on a detailed analysis of accounting ratios which we attach in an appendix.

Earnings per share have fallen from 75.1 to 0.7. This is brought about by a drop of 33⅓% in sales, a fall in the gross profit percentage, and a fall in expenses of only 13%. This situation calls for investigation and we would suggest the following lines of inquiry should be pursued:

Sales. The fall in sales is the most alarming single feature of these accounts. We wonder whether there has been any special factor affecting the business during the year, such as industrial action. If not, then it would seem advisable for the directors to consider whether the sales level can be restored to 1971 levels. The drop in profit margins and increase in advertising expenditure suggests that attempts to do this have already been made without success; if this is so, then the directors should review the present pattern of expenditure to bring it into line with the reduced level of activity.

Stock. Stock at the end of 1972 represents 230 days' sales, compared with 91 days at the end of 1971. This is particularly worrying in a high-fashion industry, and it may well be advisable to review the stock position to see whether the stock can in fact be realized at a selling price in excess of cost. The increase in the stock level must have placed a great strain on company liquidity, and the increase in bank interest probably represents the cost of bank borrowing required to finance this high stock level.

Wages and salaries. Directors' remuneration has fallen by 64%. In companies where the directors are also major shareholders it is common to distribute profits in the form of directors' emoluments, for tax reasons; if this is the case with Unigear then the fall in profitability has been even greater than is shown in the accounts.

Wages and salaries have fallen by 20%, compared with a 33% fall in the level of activity. If the level of sales cannot be increased then it will be necessary to consider reductions in staffing levels.

Repairs and renewals. The 71% fall in this category of expenditure is understandable considering the financial strains in 1972. However, expenditure of this kind cannot be cut back over a long period of time without risk of deterioration of fixed assets.

Telephone. Although a minor item of expenditure, we are puzzled by the dramatic fall in expense. We wonder whether there has been some omission in preparing the accounts, and if so whether this indicates the possibility of other error.

Bank interest. Although we do not have a balance sheet for this company, the 108% increase for this item indicates a substantial rise in borrowings. We suspect that the bank may well be reluctant to continue this level of lending in view of the 1972 accounts and, in conjunction with our views on stock expressed above, would advise the directors to take urgent action to cut the level of borrowings.

Bad debts. The 206% increase in bad debts, occurring in a year when sales dropped by a third, is very striking. If these bad debts relate to sales in 1972, we wonder whether there has been some relaxation in credit control procedures, in an attempt to increase sales; if so, this policy may need review in the light of these bad debt figures.

To summarize our conclusions, the company faces a liquidity crisis because of high levels of stock and bank borrowings. The company must either find ways of increasing the level of sales, or else bring down the level of expenses, particularly wage costs, in line with the reduced level of activity.

Appendix

Ratios

	1971		*1972*	
Gross profit %	$\dfrac{600}{1,500}$	40%	$\dfrac{350}{1,000}$	35%

Days stock	$\dfrac{300}{1,200} \times 365$	91	$\dfrac{410}{650} \times 365$	230
Stock turnover	$\dfrac{1,200}{300}$	4	$\dfrac{650}{410}$	1.6
Earnings per share	$\dfrac{150,296}{200,000}$	75.1p	$\dfrac{1,402}{200,000}$	0.7p

% movement in income and expenditure:

Sales	33⅓% decrease
Rent and rates	15.8% increase
Light and heat	37% increase
Telephone	88.3% decrease
Wages and salaries — excluding directors	19.7% decrease
Directors' remuneration	63.6% decrease
Advertising	5.9% increase
Repairs and renewals	71.2% decrease
Bad debts	206% increase
Bank interest and commission	108% increase
Audit fee	17.6% increase
General expenses	21.5% increase
Depreciation	16.7% decrease
Total expenses	13.1% decrease

Question 9: solution

(a) Calculations of stated factors:

$\dfrac{\text{Profit before tax}}{\text{Current liabilities}}$:

Go-go Products		Numerous Inventions	
1977	*1976*	*1977*	*1976*
$\dfrac{1,400}{7,930} = 0.18$	$\dfrac{935}{9,970} = 0.09$	$\dfrac{1,090}{4,357} = 0.25$	$\dfrac{1,278}{2,467} = 0.52$

$\dfrac{\text{Current assets}}{\text{Total liabilities}}$:

Go-go Products		Numerous Inventions	
1977	*1976*	*1977*	*1976*
$\dfrac{10,801}{9,339} = 1.16$	$\dfrac{11,537}{11,138} = 1.04$	$\dfrac{6,798}{4,412} = 1.54$	$\dfrac{4,859}{2,505} = 1.94$

$\dfrac{\text{Current liabilities}}{\text{Total tangible assets}}$:

Go-go Products		Numerous Inventions	
1977	*1976*	*1977*	*1976*
$\dfrac{7,930}{15,445} = 0.51$	$\dfrac{9,970}{16,765} = 0.59$	$\dfrac{4,357}{8,748} = 0.50$	$\dfrac{2,467}{6,389} = 0.39$

No credit interval:

Go-go Products		*Numerous Inventions*	
1977	*1976*	*1977*	*1976*
$\dfrac{2{,}871}{28{,}356} = 0.10$	$\dfrac{1{,}567}{24{,}198} = 0.06$	$\dfrac{2{,}441}{8{,}313} = 0.29$	$\dfrac{2{,}392}{6{,}571} = 0.36$
$= 37$ days	$= 24$ days	$= 107$ days	$= 133$ days

$$\text{Current ratio} = \frac{(\text{Current assets})}{(\text{Current liabilities})};$$

Go-go Products		*Numerous Inventions*	
1977	*1976*	*1977*	*1976*
$\dfrac{4{,}558}{7{,}930} = 0.57$	$\dfrac{4{,}764}{9{,}970} = 0.48$	$\dfrac{5{,}812}{4{,}357} = 1.33$	$\dfrac{3{,}602}{2{,}467} = 1.46$

(b) The movement of each ratio can be summarized as follows, where U = unfavourable, F = favourable.
Total tangible assets

	Go-go Products	*Numerous Inventions*
$\dfrac{\text{Profit before tax}}{\text{Current liabilities}}$	F	U
$\dfrac{\text{Current assets}}{\text{Total liabilities}}$	F	U
$\dfrac{\text{Current liabilities}}{\text{Total tangible assets}}$	F	U
No credit interval	F	U
Current ratio	F	U
Liquidity	F	U

Assuming that by 'unfavourable' we mean that the ratio indicates less cause for confidence in the going-concern status than previously, then for Go-go each ratio has moved in a favourable direction, while for Numerous each ratio has moved in an unfavourable direction. However, at 30 April 1977 each ratio for Numerous is still more favourable than for Go-go. If these two companies are operating in the same industry then the ratios will be comparable between the companies, and we can state that Numerous has a stronger liquidity position than Go-go but that Go-go is gaining strength while Numerous is deteriorating. On the other hand, if the two companies are in different industries then we cannot compare their ratios directly, and we can only compare the trends within each company.

(c) The following limitations of ratio analysis as a predictor of failure can be identified:

(i) Different companies may use different accounting policies, or change their policies from one year to another, so that accounts may not be comparable.

(ii)   In times of inflation historical cost accounts understate the value of non-monetary assets recorded in the balance sheet and consumed in the profit and loss account, distorting analysis unless current cost accounts are available.

Neither of these first limitations is too serious in the case of prediction of failure because ratios relating to liquidity draw mainly on current asset and liability figures, most of which are fixed in monetary amounts, while even the stock figure is not substantially influenced by inflation.

(iii)   Where a company is engaged in several different activities, a change in ratios may indicate a change in the 'mix' of activities rather than in the liquidity position.

(iv)   The liquidity position may be influenced by 'off balance sheet' data; for example, a bank overdraft may in substance be a form of long-term finance.

(v)   In a business with seasonal fluctuations in activity, companies with differing year ends may not be comparable and ratios may fail to show the effect of times when resources are strained.

These limitations influence the way in which the analyst uses accounting ratios, but need not mean that ratio analysis cannot predict failure. Studies have shown that ratio analysis can predict 95% of cases of corporate failure.

Tutorial note:
While based on an article in *Accountancy*, no knowledge of the article was required to answer the question; in fact, the definition of the 'no-credit interval' provided in the question is rather different to that used in the article.

Question 10: solution

New Ideas Limited

(a)   (i)   Computation of ratios:

	1976		1975	
Acid test	$\dfrac{21,856 + 2,917}{18,762 + 1,642 + 1,000} = 1.2$		$\dfrac{20,264 + 6,094}{16,431 + 1,247 + 900} = 1.4$	
Current ratio	$\dfrac{25,426 + 21,856 + 2,917}{187 + 1,642 + 1,000} = 2.3$		$\dfrac{20,231 + 20,264 + 6,094}{16,431 + 1,247 + 900} = 2.5$	

(ii)   Pre-tax return on total funds:

	$\dfrac{9,380}{56,600} = 16.6\%$		$\dfrac{8,362}{49,108} = 17\%$	
Net profit %	$\dfrac{9,380}{264,626} = 3.5\%$		$\dfrac{8,362}{220,393} = 3.8\%$	
Asset turnover	$\dfrac{264,626}{56,600} = 4.7$		$\dfrac{220,393}{49,108} = 4.5$	

(iii)   Earnings per share:

$$\frac{4,000}{10,000} = 40p \qquad\qquad \frac{3,720}{10,000} = 37.2p$$

Dividend cover $\dfrac{4,000}{1,500} = 2.7$ $\qquad\qquad \dfrac{3,720}{1,400} = 2.7$

(b)   **Brief comments on the changes in ratios:** The fall in both the acid test and the current ratio indicate a decline in the liquidity position of the company. This is not necessarily dangerous, but does warrant further investigation, for example by comparison with industrial averages.

   Return on total funds has fallen slightly. Computation of the secondary ratios shows a slight rise in asset turnover and a slight fall in the net profit percentage, suggesting possibly that an attempt to boost sales may have been accompanied by a rise in expenses.

   Earnings per share have increased, not because of increases in the return on capital but because of the increase in total resources employed. Dividend cover is constant, and the level of cover is reasonable.

(c)   Effect on gearing ratio: Long term:

Currently $\dfrac{15,433}{19,763 + 15,433} = 43.8\%$

Scheme 1 $\dfrac{31,433}{19,763 + 31,433} = 61.4\%$

Scheme 2 $\dfrac{15,433}{35,763 + 15,433} = 30.1\%$

Scheme 3 $\dfrac{31,433}{19,763 + 31,433} = 61.4\%$

(d)   Effect on earnings per share:

Current   40p

Scheme 1 — basic $\dfrac{4,950}{10,000} = 49.5p$

   fully diluted $\dfrac{5,750}{26,000} = 22.1p$

Scheme 2 $\dfrac{5,750}{30,000} = 19.2p$

Scheme 3 $\dfrac{4,710}{10,000} = 47.1p$

(e)   **Advice to management:** Scheme 1 and scheme 3 both involve a substantial increase in gearing, whereas scheme 2 involves a fall. Scheme 1 and scheme 3 both result in substantial increases in earnings per share, although scheme 1 involves a substantial fall in earnings per share when, in fourteen years' time, full dilution occurs.

   Schemes 1 and 2 both involve raising finance from existing shareholders. Providing that the borrowing powers permit, scheme 1 seems more attractive, particularly as tax relief is available on the loan interest.

Comparing scheme 1 with scheme 3, although the gearing ratios are the same, the convertible stock will not require any cash outflow on coversion, whereas the 13% debentures would have to be repaid between 1990 and 2000. Providing that shareholders find the issue of convertible loan stock attractive, scheme 1 would therefore seem preferable.

Workings:

(i) Profit and loss account:

	1976	1975
Trading profit	9,380	8,362
Interest	1,000	1,000
Profit before tax	8,380	9,362
Taxation	4,380	3,642
Profit after tax	4,000	3,720
Dividends	1,500	1,400
Retained profit	2,500	2,320

(ii) Long-term funds employed:

	At present £000	Scheme 1 £000	Scheme 2 £000	Scheme 3 £000
Ordinary shares	5,000	5,000	15,000	5,000
Share premium	—	—	—	—
Revenue reserves	14,763	14,763	14,763	14,763
	19,763	19,763	35,763	19,763
Deferred tax	5,433	5,433	5,433	5,433
10% Debentures	10,000	10,000	10,000	10,000
Convertible stock	—	16,000	—	—
13% Debentures	—	—	—	16,000
	15,433	31,433	15,433	31,433

(iii) Earnings under each scheme:

	£000	Scheme 1 £000	Scheme 2 £000	Scheme 3 £000
Current trading profit		9,380	9,380	9,380
New income		3,500	3,500	3,500
		12,880	12,880	12,880
Interest: Current	1,000	1,000	1,000	1,000
New	1,600	2,600	— 1,000	2,080 3,080
Profit before tax		10,280	11,880	9,800
Tax: Current	4,380	4,380	4,380	4,380
at 50% on new income less interest	950	1,750 5,330	710 6,130	5,090
		4,950	5,750	4,710

Fully diluted earnings under scheme 1 will be the same as earnings under scheme 2.

Tutorial note:
Clearly, a range of ratios could have been given in answer to part (a). Gearing ratios could have been computed with reference either to total or long-term funds employed.

Question 11: solution

Northern Manufacturing Co Ltd

(a) Earnings per share:

	1979	1978
Basic	16.2p	11.2p
Fully diluted	13.2p	9.7p

(b) Price/earnings ratio:

Currently $\dfrac{£1.80}{16.2p} = 11.1$

High $\dfrac{£2.00}{16.2p} = 12.3$

Low $\dfrac{£1.10}{16.2p} = 6.8$

(c) Ratios relating to liquidity:

	1979	1978
Current ratio	$\dfrac{1,800}{1,000} = 1.8$	$\dfrac{1,140}{540} = 2.1$
Acid test	$\dfrac{800}{1,000} = 0.8$	$\dfrac{540}{540} = 1$
Stock turnover	$\dfrac{7,000}{1,000} = 7$	$\dfrac{5,000}{600} = 8.3$
Days debtors	$\dfrac{800}{7,000} \times 365 = 41$	$\dfrac{500}{5,000} \times 365 = 36$

(d) There has been some decline in both the current ratio and the acid test during the year. The fall in stock turnover and the rise in the number of days debtors suggest an increased demand for working capital in relation to the level of activity. The working capital position is highlighted if we extract the working capital items from the funds statement:

	1979 £000	1978 £000
Movement in working capital:		
Increase in debtors	300	100
Increase in stock	400	200
Increase in creditors	(350)	(100)
	350	300

Net liquid funds/decrease	(150)	—
Net inflow of funds in year	200	300

Liquidity is also under pressure because of other applications of funds. New plant purchases substantially exceed funds raised from the share issue, while dividend and ACT payments together have doubled in 1979.

Clearly, for this company the bank overdraft is in substance a form of long-term borrowing, and in view of the fluctuations over the years need not necessarily cause concern. However, the doubling of trade creditors in the year, together with the stock turnover and debtors' position, should cause this company to give some throught to its working capital management.

Workings:

(a)   Earnings per share:

Basic — 1978:

$$\frac{£67,000}{600,000} = 11.2p$$

1979:

$$\frac{£140,000}{(600,000 \times 1/3) + (1,000,000 \times 2/3)} = 16.2p$$

Diluted — 1978:

$$\frac{£67,000 + £40,000}{600,000 + 500,000} = 9.7p$$

1979:

$$\frac{£140,000 + £40,000}{(600,000 \times 1/3) + (1,000,000 \times 2/3) + 500,000} = 13.2p$$

Tutorial note:
On the computational side, this is an example of a question where the lack of information (in this case the market price of shares at the date of the share issue) forces the student to make an assumption.

A wealth of information was made available for part (d), and many different approaches were possible. Note that the funds statement and the ratios were both valuable sources of evidence.

Question 12: solution

A. General engineering:
This ties in with company 2, showing high investment in plant and machinery (other fixed assets) and high stock and work-in-progress, debtors, and creditors.

B. Investment in properties for rental:

This ties in with company 8, very high land and property investment, no stock, low plant, debtors, and creditors. High bank overdraft is slightly surprising — although we expect high gearing, borrowings would normally be longer term.

C. Estate development and house builders:

This ties in with company 3 — high stock and work-in-progress, low fixed assets, some bank borrowing. (Note: Land will be held as stock, not fixed asset.)

D. Whisky distillers and blenders:

This ties in with company 7 — high stock of whisky maturing — reasonable land and building for storage — finance from creditors and the bank kept down.

E. Brewers:

This ties with company 1 — high land and buildings (brewery and tied houses), reasonable plant and machinery, stock and debtors low compared to creditors.

F. Retail stores:

This ties in with company 6 — high property investment, very low debtors, stock financed by creditors, surplus cash in hand.

G. Conglomerate with various activities:

This ties in with company 4 — investment in various trades produces averaging of ratios so that none stand out.

H. Insurance brokers:

This ties in with company 5 — no stock and work-in-progress, high debtors and creditors to be expected in this kind of agency work, combination of high investments and bank overdraft to be expected from finance brokerage of this kind.

Tutorial note:

A question that uses common sense rather than specific ratio analysis techniques.

Question 13: solution

1. The term gearing, when applied to the capital structure of a company, refers to the relationship between finance supplied by the proprietors of the business and finance supplied from other sources.

    A 'low-geared' company has a high proportion of its finance supplied by the proprietors, while a 'high-geared' company has a small proportion of its finance supplied by the proprietors.

    Gearing has a significant effect both on the income of the shareholders and the financial risks run by the company. Those who lend money to a company receive a fixed consideration, normally in the form of interest payments, for the use of the finance they supply, and this consideration does not fluctuate with the level of profit, the proprietors are entitled to the residue of profit after the claims of lenders have been met. Where a company is highly geared there will be a large fixed claim upon the operating profit to meet interest payments, so that any fluctuation in the operating profit will lead to a proportionally far higher fluctuation in the profit available to share-holders. Financial risk increases with higher gearing for two reasons:

(a) The obligation to make interest payments irrespective of the level of profits means that in bad trading years there will still be a heavy outflow of cash to those who have financed the business.

(b) If over a period of time losses accumulate, then the more highly geared the company the more rapidly will the proprietors' interest be eroded, so that loans cannot be repaid in full.

A business venture would normally be expected to earn a rate of return in excess of current interest rates, since otherwise the resources of the business would be lent out rather than employed internally, thus, when a company borrows money equity shareholders might expect to benefit from the excess of the return earned over the related interest payments. When planning the capital structure of a company it is necessary to balance this benefit against the risks of gearing.

2. 'Concealed gearing' arises where part of the resources of the business are financed by third parties in a way that is not reflected in the balance sheet. Two examples are:

(a) **Leasing plant and machinery.** Where a business enters into a lease agreement, acquiring the right to use plant and machinery, traditional accounting practice involves recording the lease pay-ments as an expense in the profit and loss account. However, where a lease is entered into for the major part of the life of an asset the commercial substance of the transaction is that the asset has been acquired by the business with finance supplied by the lessor. The commitment to make regular lease payments is a fixed claim on the company's profit in the same way as making interest payments on a loan.

(b) **Factoring debtors.** Where the right to collect amounts due from debtors is sold, the transaction may be similar in character to a loan raised on the security of debtors, but neither the asset nor the liability will be shown in the accounts.

Such sources of finance are often referred to as 'off balance sheet' finance.

3. The various ratios computed below show that if preference shares are regarded as part of the proprietors' interest then Gamma Ltd is more highly geared, while if preference shares are regarded as a form of borrowing Alpha Ltd is more highly geared.

There are arguments for each approach to preference shares. On the one hand, preference shares are in law a form of share capital, pre-ference dividends may only be paid out of profits, and in the event of a liquidation no repayment is made to preference shareholders until all creditors have been satisfied in full. Thus, from the point of view of creditors assessing the risk of lending to a company, gearing ratios that treat preference shares as part of the proprietors' interests seem the best measure. On the other hand, preference shareholders only receive a fixed level of dividend irrespective of the level of profits, and have a claim to receive their dividend in full before any payment is made to other shareholders. Therefore, from the point of view of equity share-holders assessing the impact of gearing on fluctuations in their share of profit, it seems more appropriate to regard preference shares as a form of borrowing. Thus we can only answer the question as to which company is more highly geared if we know the reasons why the question is being asked.

Gearing ratios:

Treating preference shares as part of proprietor's interest:

	Alpha Ltd	*Gamma Ltd*
$\dfrac{\text{Borrowings}}{\text{Total funds}}$	$\dfrac{-}{3,000,000} = 0\%$	$\dfrac{60,000}{3,000,000} = 20\%$
Interest cover	—	$\dfrac{800,000}{48,000} = 16\frac{2}{3}$
Degree of capital gearing	1	$\dfrac{800,000}{752,000} = 1.064$

Treating preference shares as a form of borrowing:

$\dfrac{\text{Borrowings}}{\text{Total funds}}$	$\dfrac{1,800,000}{3,000,000} = 60\%$	$\dfrac{1,500,000}{3,000,000} = 50\%$
Fixed charge cover	$\dfrac{800,000}{113,400^*} = 7$	$\dfrac{800,000}{56,700 + 4,800^*} = 7.6$
Degree of capital gearing	$\dfrac{800,000}{686,600^*} = 1.165$	$\dfrac{800,000}{695,300^*} = 1.15$

(* In the absence of information on rates of taxation, taxation has been ignored. If the information were available, we would adjust the pre-ference dividend in computing these ratios by the factor:

$$\frac{1}{1 - \text{Corporation tax rate}}$$

This adjustment is necessary in order to reflect the amount of pre-tax profit that has to be earned in order to cover the preference dividend.)

Tutorial note:

This question requires students to show an understanding of the different ways in which preference shares can be regarded. Note how the problem of lack of data on the tax rate can be handled — making a note to the examiner that shows that the student is aware of the problems involved.

Question 14: solution

1. The price earnings ratio, computed as:

$$\frac{\text{Share price}}{\text{Earnings per share}}$$

expresses the relationship between the stock market price of a share and the earnings after tax and before extraordinary items attributable to that share. Thus the analyst can see what multiple of earnings the share price represents.

The dividend yield, computed as:

$$\frac{\text{Dividend per share}}{\text{Share price}}$$

expresses the percentage return that an investor in ordinary shares would currently earn on that investment in the form of dividend.

The stock turnover ratio can be computed as:

$$\frac{\text{Cost of sales}}{\text{Stock}}$$

and in this case represents the number of times stock turns over during the year, assuming that stock levels do not fluctuate. The ratio may also be computed as:

$$\frac{\text{Turnover}}{\text{Stock}}$$

Since stock is measured at cost, while turnover is measured at selling price, this ratio is not as useful as one based on cost of sales. Whichever way the ratio is computed, it expresses the relationship between the quantity of stock held and the level of activity.

Pre-tax return on capital employed, computed as:

$$\frac{\text{Pre-tax return}}{\text{Capital}}$$

expresses the relationship between the profit earned by a business and the resources it employs.

'Capital' can be defined in a number of ways, including:

(a) **Shareholders' equity.** In this case return will be profit before tax.
(b) **Long-term funds employed.** In this case return will be profit before tax plus long-term interest.
(c) **Total funds employed.** In this case return will be profit before tax plus total interest.

When the term 'return on capital employed' is used on its own without further definition, it normally refers to either long-term or total funds.

2. The P/E ratio indicates that investors in the dairy-food industry value the 'earnings' of those companies more highly than investors in the

building-materials industry; this is turn suggests that the stock market has more confidence in the future prospects of dairy-food retailing.

The lower dividend yield in dairy-food retailing appears to be attributable to two factors:

(a) Share prices in the industry are higher relative to earnings.
(b) The industry is distributing a lower proportion of earnings as dividends. This may well be because there are better prospects in that industry, and therefore better opportunities to employ retained profits. This view is supported both by the P/E ratio and the return on capital employed.

Stock turnover in dairy-foods retailing is very much faster than in the building-materials industry. We would expect this because:

(a) Dairy-food retailing involves many perishable products, which cannot be held for long periods of time.
(b) Dairy-food sales are likely to occur at an even and reasonably predictable rate. By contrast, building materials cover a wide range of product lines with a less even and predictable pattern of demand.

Differing rates of stock turnover are, therefore, to be expected and tell us nothing about the current state of the industry.

The pre-tax return on capital employed is comparable between industries, and in this case indicates that currently the dairy-food retailing industry is operating more profitably than the building-materials industry. The building-materials industry is subject to greater fluctuations in demand over the years, and it would seem likely that at the time when these industrial averages were computed the industry was in a relatively depressed state.

Tutorial note:
When describing the meaning of a ratio it is not sufficient simply to describe how the ratio is computed, although such a description is likely to form part of the explanation.

Question 15: solution

1. Earnings per share:

Net basis	$\dfrac{4,360}{15,000} = 29.1\text{p}$
Nil basis	$\dfrac{4,860}{15,000} = 32.4\text{p}$

P/E ratio:

Net basis	$\dfrac{220}{29.1} = 7.6$
Nil basis	$\dfrac{220}{32.4} = 6.8$

Dividend yield:

Dividends per share	$\dfrac{3,500}{15,000} = 23.3\text{p}$
Dividend yield	$\dfrac{23.3}{220} = 10.6\%$

2. The P/E ratio expresses the relationship between the share price and the earnings per share. The earnings figure is based on profit after taxation and before extraordinary items, and therefore reflects the results of the ordinary activities of the business. Potential investors can therefore see from the P/E ratio what multiple of earnings the share price represents. When a company shows a high P/E ratio, this suggests that the stock market expects a growth in future earnings; conversely, a low P/E ratio suggests that the market does not have confidence in a company's ability to maintain the current level of earnings.

    The dividend yield expresses the dividend per share as a percentage of the share price. It tells the potential investor what rate of return he would receive in the form of dividends on the basis of the most recent accounting year. Starting from this basis the analyst will try and estimate whether future dividends are likely to increase or decrease, based on a review of performance ratios, dividend cover, estimates of future cash flow, and evidence of the company's dividend policy.

3. Earnings per share on the net basis are computed with reference to profit after the actual tax charge shown in the accounts. Earnings per share on the nil basis are computed with reference to profit after tax charge excluding irrecoverable advance corporation tax (ACT). The argument for the nil basis is that irrecoverable ACT arises from the payment of dividends, and since dividend policy may vary from year to year and from company to company the nil basis gives a more comparable earnings figure. The net basis, on the other hand, reflects the actual earnings available to shareholders. Each basis may be more appropriate in different circumstances and therefore it is good practice to disclose both, where material, as provided in SSAP 3.

Question 16: solution

Ballindine Ltd

A comparison of some accounting ratios for 1982, the 1983 budget, and 1983, presents at first sight a rather puzzling picture. The company has apparently planned to allow the current ratio and liquidity ratio to drop dramatically in 1983, and the actual fall has been even greater than planned. The company has apparently planned to allow the number of days debtors to rise by 50% and the rate of stock turnover to drop by one-third and the actual movement has been even greater. The company has planned for a drop in the return on capital employed, and experienced a greater fall than planned.

The budget indicates that the company has planned:

(a)   Substantial additions to plant — representing either replacement of worn-out machinery or an expansion of capacity.

(b)   Doubling of stock and debtors — representing either a relaxation in stock and credit control or an expansion in activity.

(c)   Doubling of creditors — representing slower payment or increased purchases.

(d)   An increase in sales — which could represent a steady increase during the year or a more dramatic increase in the latter part of the year.

(e)   Increased rent and rates — suggesting cost increases, or a plan to expand the amount of the premises occupied.

(f)   Trebled advertising expenditure — suggesting a plan to boost sales substantially.

Thus all the evidence is consistent with a plan to expand productive capacity and consequently increase sales in the latter part of the year.

The actual results for 1983 indicate one major change in this plan — the acquisition of new land and buildings, no doubt related to a reduction in rent and rates compared to budget. This has been financed in part by the issue of the debentures, apparently issued halfway through the year since only one-halfyear's interest is charged against profit. The turnover figure may well be lower than budgeted because of some delay in launching the new production.

The auditor would hold discussions with management to confirm this impression of planned expansion. Stock control and credit control could then be judged by reference to sales and purchases in the final month rather than the final year.

Additional audit work would be necessary in relation to fixed assets and the debenture issue; it should be borne in mind that the company's borrowing powers should be checked relating to the latter.

Assuming a dramatic expansion of the company's operations, it is necessary to consider whether the internal control system is adequate for the new workload.

Finally, in view of the level of the overdraft compared with the budget, the validity of the going-concern concept should be considered. This would involve considering the agreed overdraft limit, the cash budgets, and consideration of developments after the balance sheet date.

Accounting ratios:

	1982 *Actual*	*1983* *Budgeted*	*1983* *Actual*
Current ratio	$\dfrac{130}{30} = 4.3$	$\dfrac{160}{75} = 2.1$	$\dfrac{160}{127} = 1.3$
Liquidity ratio	$\dfrac{100}{30} = 3.3$	$\dfrac{100}{75} = 1.3$	$\dfrac{100}{127} = 0.8$
Stock turn	$\dfrac{360}{30} = 12$	$\dfrac{480}{60} = 8$	$\dfrac{420}{60} = 7$

Days debtors	$\dfrac{50}{600} \times 365 = 30.4$	$\dfrac{100}{800} \times 365 = 45.6$	$\dfrac{100}{700} \times 365 = 52.1$
Return on long-term funds	$\dfrac{70}{250} = 28\%$	$\dfrac{55}{305} = 18\%$	$\dfrac{23 + 3}{333} = 8\%$
Gross profit %	$\dfrac{240}{600} = 40\%$	$\dfrac{320}{800} = 40\%$	$\dfrac{280}{700} = 40\%$
Net profit %	$\dfrac{70}{600} = 11.7\%$	$\dfrac{55}{800} = 6.9\%$	$\dfrac{26}{700} = 3.7\%$
Asset turnover	$\dfrac{600}{250} = 2.4$	$\dfrac{800}{305} = 2.6$	$\dfrac{700}{333} = 2.1$

Question 17: solution

Report to the Finance Director of GIV Manufacturing Ltd

The following analysis of the company's financial strategy is based on an examination of key ratios for the five-year period of 1976–80.

(a) **The company's management of working capital:** Over the five years the company's turnover has increased by 85%, compared to an industrial average of 50%. Such an increase in turnover leads to a demand for increased working capital. There are a number of ways in which a company can respond to such a requirement:

(i) By stricter control of stock and debtors. In this case the number of days debtors dropped slightly in 1977, but increased substantially in each of the following three years. The number of days stockholding fell in 1977 and 1978, but was allowed to rise in 1979 and 1980 to a point eight days higher than in 1976. Thus there appears to have been some attempt to solve the problem of an increased working capital requirement by tighter control of debtors in 1977, and stock in both 1977 and 1978, but in later years this process has been reversed so that in addition to the increase in working capital resulting from increased turnover, a further increase has been caused by relaxed stock control and credit control.

(ii) By increased short-term borrowing. In this case the number of days creditors has only fluctuated slightly, while the current and liquid ratios have actually increased. Thus we can see that the company has tended to avoid this response, although the fall in the current and liquid ratios in 1978 suggests that there may have been some erosion of cash holdings, or increase in short-term borrowings, in that year.

(iii) By increased long-term borrowing. Both measures of leverage have fallen substantially over the five years, suggesting either some loan repayments or an increase in equity, or possibly a combination of the two.

(iv) By retaining funds generated from operations in the business, and using these to finance the increased working capital requirement. This approach is suggested by the company's dividend payout percentage, which is so much lower than the industrial average, while the company is more profitable than the industrial average. Such an explanation is also consistent with the points considered in (iii) above.

(b) **Share price trends:** Over the five-year period share prices for the industry have increased, and the company has performed better than the industrial average. Table 1 shows how in 1977 and 1978 the share price rose ahead of the industry, while in 1979 and 1980 share prices fell more sharply than average.

Table 1   Share price movement

	1977	1978	1979	1980
Company	50% +	33% +	20% −	19% −
Industry	10% +	18% +	8% −	8% −

At first sight the company's share price seems to be more volatile than the industrial average. However, gearing is low and falling, while the dividend payout is half the industrial average, suggesting cautious management. It would seem appropriate, therefore, to look for aspects of the company's performance that would be regarded favourably in the first half of the five-year period, and unfavourably in the second half.

Table 2 shows the increase in sales each year for the company and for the industry, based on the sales index figures. In 1977 and 1978 the company has performed better than average, in 1979 it is exactly in line with the average, and in 1980 it falls well behind the rest of industry. It is interesting to observe that the substantial increase in days debtors and inventory during 1979 and 1980 have not been linked to any success in expanding the company's market share.

Table 2   Sales increase

	1977	1978	1979	1980
Company	20%	33%	12.5%	3%
Industry	10%	9%	12.5%	11%

In 1977 the company's return on net worth fell sharply, but remained well ahead of the industrial average.

In 1979 and 1980 the ratio has fallen again, to a point close to the industrial average. Thus the company, having led the industry in expanding turnover and in profitability, is now lagging behind the industry in expanding turnover and is only just ahead with its return on net worth.

In explaining the share price it is also important to consider the level of dividends. Shareholders may well have been happy to accept low dividend payouts when the company led the industry in expanding turnover and profitability; such a policy is far less acceptable in a company lagging behind the rest of the industry.

We can now construct a broad picture of GIV Manufacturing Ltd having retained a higher proportion of funds generated from operations in the business than is usual in this industry; the management have allowed these resources to be absorbed by debtors and stock, partly because of increased turnover but also because of weak working capital control. This unproductive use of resources has led to a substantial fall in the return on net worth. The stock market has taken the view that there is little attraction in a company that has a low dividend yield and is not able to compensate with effective use of retained profits. We are told that management 'feels content', and this complacency is typical of the way in which they have conducted the company's affairs.

Conclusion

One of the dangers of using retained profits as a source of finance is that their cost is not immediately apparent to management, only being reflected, as in this case, by the response of the share price to inefficient use. Nevertheless, the company has considerable strengths. Return on net worth is still ahead of the industry; tightening up the control over stock and debtors could release substantial resources, and the low level of gearing gives the company the opportunity to raise new long-term borrowings. The share price is still ahead of the industrial average, suggesting that the market is aware of disappointments in the past but also of opportunities for the future.

Tutorial note:

An interesting question, which wastes none of the student's time in the mechanical exercise of computing ratios. On a year-to-year basis changes are undramatic, and it is necessary to consider trends over the five years to get a clear picture.

Question 18: solution

Karri-Krane — Report to the Chairman

This review of the company's financial position over the past five years is based on the accounting ratios that are attached in Table 1.

Clearly, the plant expansion programme undertaken during 1976 has been the major factor affecting the company's development during the five years. The programme was apparently undertaken approximately halfway through that year, since during 1976 only six months' interest was charged on the loan stock in that year.

From 1974 to 1975 the current ratio and acid test remained steady, but over the next three years there is a material and accelerating drop in these

Table 1 Karri-Krane

	1978	1977	1976	1975	1974
Current ratio	$\dfrac{9,400}{5,700} = 1.65$	$\dfrac{7,700}{4,100} = 1.88$	$\dfrac{6,875}{3,325} = 2.07$	$\dfrac{5,825}{2,775} = 2.10$	$\dfrac{5,325}{2,525} = 2.11$
Acid test	$\dfrac{9,400 - 3,500}{5,700} = 1.04$	$\dfrac{7,700 - 3,000}{4,100} = 1.15$	$\dfrac{6,875 - 2,800}{3,325} = 1.23$	$\dfrac{5,825 - 2,300}{2,775} = 1.31$	$\dfrac{5,325 - 2,000}{2,525} = 1.32$
Gearing: Long-term	$\dfrac{4,250}{12,700} = 33.5\%$	$\dfrac{4,100}{12,200} = 33.6\%$	$\dfrac{3,900}{11,900} = 32.8\%$	$\dfrac{1,420}{9,000} = 15.8\%$	$\dfrac{1,300}{8,600} = 15.1\%$
Total	$\dfrac{4,250 + 5,700}{12,700 + 5,700} = 54.1\%$	$\dfrac{4,100 + 4,100}{12,200 + 4,100} = 50.3\%$	$\dfrac{3,900 + 3,325}{11,900 + 3,325} = 47.5\%$	$\dfrac{1,420 + 2,775}{9,900 + 2,775} = 37.2\%$	$\dfrac{1,300 + 2,525}{8,600 + 2,525} = 34.4\%$
Return on:					
Shareholders' funds	$\dfrac{1,744}{8,450} = 20.1\%$	$\dfrac{1,244}{8,100} = 15.4\%$	$\dfrac{1,874}{8,000} = 23.4\%$	$\dfrac{1,604}{7,580} = 21.2\%$	$\dfrac{1,254}{7,300} = 17.2\%$
Long-term funds	$\dfrac{2,100}{12,700} = 16.5\%$	$\dfrac{1,600}{12,200} = 13.1\%$	$\dfrac{2,100}{11,900} = 17.6\%$	$\dfrac{1,700}{9,000} = 18.9\%$	$\dfrac{1,350}{8,600} = 15.7\%$
Asset/turnover	$\dfrac{23,500}{12,700} = 1.85$	$\dfrac{21,000}{12,200} = 1.72$	$\dfrac{19,000}{11,900} = 1.50$	$\dfrac{16,800}{9,000} = 1.87$	$\dfrac{15,000}{8,600} = 1.74$
Net profit	$\dfrac{2,100}{23,500} = 8.9\%$	$\dfrac{1,600}{21,000} = 7.6\%$	$\dfrac{2,100}{19,000} = 11\%$	$\dfrac{1,700}{16,800} = 10.2\%$	$\dfrac{1,350}{15,000} = 9\%$

ratios. Thus it would appear that the increased turnover that has resulted from the expansion programme has led to an increased working capital requirement that has not been met in full from long-term borrowings or retained profits. If the company continues to be unable to finance increased working capital requirements from long-term sources then there may be liquidity problems in the near future.

Gearing rose substantially during 1976, as we might expect as a result of the plant expansion programme in that year. During 1977 and 1978 gearing measured in relation to total borrowings has continued to rise, because of the reliance on short-term borrowings to finance working capital requirements. Because the company has been able to earn a rate of return on funds employed in excess of the rate of interest paid, this increase in gearing has helped to boost the return on shareholders' funds. Thus if we compare 1974 to 1978 there has been an increase of 0.8% in the return on long-term funds, but an increase of 2.9% in the return on equity. The effect of increased gearing has been to make the return on equity subject to more violent fluctuations; for example in 1977 a 4.5% drop in the return on long-term funds led to an 8% drop in the return on equity. The steady increase in total borrowings as a proportion of total funds is likely to make it more difficult for the company to raise new loans in the future, a particularly worrying point when we remember that there are indications of potential liquidity problems.

The return on long-term funds rose during 1975, fell slightly in 1976 and sharply in 1977, recovering in 1978 but not returning to the 1975 level. A clearer picture emerges if we look at the secondary ratios. Asset turnover has fluctuated very moderately over four of the five years and the one exception in 1976 probably reflects the fact that a large part of the assets shown in the balance sheet at the end of that year had only been in use for part of the year. Thus we can see that over the five years the company has consistently been able to increase sales in line with increased assets employed. However, the net profit percentage, representing the return earned on sales, increased until 1976, dropped sharply in 1977, and has only recovered partially in 1978. Therefore, in order to improve profitability it would seem appropriate to consider whether profit margins on sales can be improved and to look closely at controls over expenses.

In conclusion, the company's most urgent need is to find ways to improve liquidity, and in view of recent increases in gearing it may be difficult to secure long-term borrowings for this purpose.

Question 19: solution

Tapsave Ltd

(a)

	Industrial average	1978	1977
Gross profit %	34%	32%	32%
Current ratio	2.5	2.4	2.4
Acid test	1.2	1	1.1

Average age of debtors	30 days	37 days	32 days
Stock turnover	5×	3.9×	4.9×
Interest earned	8×	5×	6.7×
Debt/equity ratio	0.7:1	1.36:1	0.89:1
Net profit before tax to net assets	19.5%	29.8%	26.4%

(b) The debt equity ratio indicates that the company's gearing is well above the industrial average. This has resulted in an interest cover ratio well below the industrial average. At the same time, the return on shareholders' funds is well above the industrial average and, since the gross profit percentage is slightly below average, it is likely that this favourable position is attributable to the high level of gearing. Since we are informed that this industry is liable to wide-ranging fluctuations in sales and profits, it would seem unwise to recommend a further increase in gearing and accordingly we would recommend rejection of the proposal to issue further debentures.

An examination of the working capital activity ratios reveals that the levels of stock and of debtors in relation to the level of the company's activity have both risen sharply during the year, while the 1977 figures were close to the industrial average. As a result there has been a fall in the acid test ratio, indicating potential liquidity problems.

The apparent weakness in working capital control, together with the gross profit percentage being slightly below average, suggests that management may have been less effective in running the operations of the business than their competitors; the impact of this on profits available to shareholders has been obscured by the effects of gearing. With tighter control of working capital substantial resources could be released to enable the company to meet its needs for additional finance. For example, if stock turnover and debt collection were brought into line with the industrial average the following funds would be released:

	£000	£000
Current stock level	5,100	
Stock level if in line with industry	$\dfrac{10,000}{5} = 3,200$	
	1,900
Current debtors level	2,900	
Level if in line with industry	$\dfrac{30}{365} \times 23,500 =$ at 1,930	
		970
Total savings		2,870

If additional finance was still required, then a share issue would seem more appropriate than a debenture issue. If new shares are to be issued, then a bonus issue may well be desirable since share capital currently forms a very small proportion of total equity, and accordingly the share price is likely to be 'heavy'.

Workings:

	1978	1977
Gross profit %	$\dfrac{7{,}500}{23{,}500} = 32\%$	$\dfrac{6{,}500}{20{,}500} = 32\%$
Current ratio	$\dfrac{8{,}700}{3{,}600} = 2.4$	$\dfrac{5{,}790}{2{,}400} = 2.4$
Acid test	$\dfrac{8{,}700 - 5{,}100}{3{,}600} = 1$	$\dfrac{5{,}790 - 3{,}200}{2{,}400} = 1.1$

Average age of debtors:

Average debtors	$\dfrac{2{,}900 + 1{,}900}{2} = 2{,}400$	$\dfrac{1{,}900 + 1{,}700}{2} = 1{,}800$
	$\dfrac{2{,}400}{23{,}500} \times 365 = 37$ days	$\dfrac{1{,}800}{20{,}500} \times 365 = 32$ days

Stock turnover:

Average stock	$\dfrac{5{,}100 + 3{,}200}{2} = 4{,}150$	$\dfrac{3{,}200 + 2{,}500}{2} = 2{,}850$
	$\dfrac{16{,}000}{4{,}150} = 3.9$	$\dfrac{14{,}000}{2{,}850} = 4.9$
Interest earned	$\dfrac{2{,}500}{500} = 5$	$\dfrac{2{,}000}{300} = 6.7$
Debt/equity ratio	$\dfrac{3{,}600 + 5{,}500}{6{,}715} = 1.36$	$\dfrac{2{,}400 + 3{,}300}{6{,}400} = 0.89$
Net profit %	$\dfrac{2{,}000}{6{,}715} = 29.8\%$	$\dfrac{1{,}700}{6{,}440} = 26.4\%$

Tutorial note:
The acid test has been computed by excluding stock from current assets. It would be possible to argue that prepayments should also be excluded since these are shown as being less liquid than stock. Debtors and stock turnover are computed in relation to average figures because the examiner has made a point of giving us the information to do this, and telling us to use it. Note that the information given to us in the preamble to the question is very important to the way we analyse the ratios.

Question 20: solution

Peak Canning Co Ltd

(a) **Ratios:**

	Industrial average	1973	1974	1975
Quick ratio	1.0	2.1	1.0	0.6
Current ratio	2.7	4.2	2.6	1.8

Stock turnover	7.0×	6.9×	4.3×	1.8×
Average collection period	32 days	34 days	37 days	50 days
Fixed asset turnover	13.0	11.6	10.7	12.4
Total asset turnover	2.6×	3.2×	2.6×	1.9×
Return on total assets	19%	24.3%	13%	5.6%
Return on net worth	36%	31.4%	19.3%	10.8%
Debt ratio	50%	22.8%	33.1%	48.2%
Profit margin on sales	7.0%	7.7%	5%	2.9%

(b) **Strengths and weaknesses:** The overall picture given by an analysis of Peak Canning's ratios over three years is alarming, with declining profitability, declining liquidity, and a sharp increase in gearing.

By contrast, the 1973 position compared with the industrial average looked healthy. Return on total assets was substantially higher than average, while the lower return on net worth figure was clearly attributable to lower gearing. Solvency ratios were well above the industrial average.

Over the three years there has been a sharp drop both in the profit margin on sales and in asset turnover. The former is attributable to a rise in expenses, since the gross profit percentage has remained constant at 20%. The rise in expenses will be partly attributable to interest charges on the bank overdraft, and also to the increased depreciation charge. It would be useful to have a more detailed breakdown of the expense figures. The drop in total asset turnover can be explored more fully. Fixed asset turnover has remained close to the industrial average and has improved in 1975; clearly the problems lie in the management of working capital. The average collection period of debtors has risen by almost 50%, and compares very unfavourably with the industrial average. Stock turnover at 1.8, compared with an industrial average of 7.0, is even more dramatically an indicator that the resources of the business are being tied up in working capital without contributing to an increase in the level of activity.

The financial director's proposals for increased borrowing, presumably to finance an even higher level of working capital, do not seem appropriate in the light of this analysis. Instead, the company should be considering ways of reducing its borrowing by tighter stock control and more prompt collection from debtors. Given that it has been possible to maintain the fixed asset turnover and the gross profit percentage, the company's weaknesses can be identified as lying in the area of working capital control.

Workings:

	1973	*1974*	*1975*
Quick ratio	$\dfrac{765,000 - 382,500}{183,600}$	$\dfrac{1,020,000 - 637,500}{392,700}$	$\dfrac{1,542,800 - 1,032,800}{836,400}$
Current ratio	$\dfrac{765,000}{183,600}$	$\dfrac{1,020,000}{392,700}$	$\dfrac{1,542,800}{836,400}$

Stock turnover	$\dfrac{2,652,000}{382,500}$	$\dfrac{2,754,000}{637,500}$	$\dfrac{2,856,000}{1,032,800}$
Average collection period	$\dfrac{306,000}{3,315,000} \times 365$	$\dfrac{346,800}{3,442,500} \times 365$	$\dfrac{484,500}{3,570,000} \times 365$
Fixed asset turnover	$\dfrac{3,315,000}{285,600}$	$\dfrac{3,442,500}{321,300}$	$\dfrac{3,570,000}{288,100}$
Total asset turnover	$\dfrac{3,315,000}{1,050,600}$	$\dfrac{3,442,500}{1,341,300}$	$\dfrac{3,570,000}{1,830,900}$
Return on total assets	$\dfrac{255,000}{1,050,600}$	$\dfrac{173,400}{1,341,300}$	$\dfrac{102,000}{1,830,900}$
Return on net worth	$\dfrac{255,000}{810,900}$	$\dfrac{173,400}{897,600}$	$\dfrac{102,000}{948,600}$
Debt ratio	$\dfrac{183,600 + 56,100}{1,050,600}$	$\dfrac{392,700 + 51,000}{1,341,300}$	$\dfrac{836,400 + 45,900}{1,830,900}$
Profit margin on sales	$\dfrac{255,000}{3,315,000}$	$\dfrac{173,400}{3,442,500}$	$\dfrac{102,000}{3,570,000}$

Assumptions made in computing ratios:

1. That stock turnover is computed by reference to cost of sales rather than sales.
2. That return on total assets and net worth are computed by reference to pre-tax profit.
3. That since no interest figure is given, interest cannot be added back to profit in computing return on total assets.

Tutorial note:
A large part of this question consisted of the requirement to compute the specified ratios. Two problems arose here:

(a) The terminology used was not adequate, in the case of some ratios, to identify precisely how the industrial average had been computed. The assumptions used were therefore listed, and were chosen because:
   (i)   Where a cost of sales figure is given, this provides a more meaningful stock turnover ratio.
   (ii) Pre-tax return figures are generally more comparable than after-tax figures.
(b) Because the interest charge was not given, the return on total assets figure cannot be computed in the normal way. Therefore the information given has been used to give the best approximation.

The analysis of the ratios was reasonably straightforward. Note that the clear trend of loss of control of working capital conflicted with the finance director's proposal to finance working capital requirements with more borrowing.

Question 21: solution

Notes in reply to Uncle Herbert

All ratios referred to in preparing these notes are listed below.

Uncle Herbert's equation can be rephrased by computing the P/E ratio, which expresses the relationship between the share price and earnings per share. This ratio is 5.5 for Cotton Value Ltd and 14.9 for Engels & Althorpe. Therefore it would appear that the stock market 'values' the earnings of Engels & Althorpe almost three times as highly as those of Cotton Value. Accordingly it seems appropriate to undertake a ratio analysis exercise in order to form a view as to why shareholders regard Engels & Althorpe as so much more promising a company.

Both companies have very low current and acid test ratios; this is normal in the retail trade. In both companies there is some increase in the acid test and little change in the current ratio. The particularly low current ratio in the case of Engels & Althorpe is indicative of tight working capital control, which is further evidenced by the high stock turnover ratio. In view of the high cash and bank balances of Engels & Althorpe the low current ratio is not a cause for concern.

Long-term borrowings are low in both companies, particularly Cotton Value. In both companies current liabilities represent a substantial proportion of total financing. In the case of Cotton Value, interest cover has dropped rather alarmingly and this may cause concern.

In 1980 Cotton Value had a substantially lower return on capital than Engels & Althorpe and in 1981 has suffered a more severe decline. In both years Engels & Althorpe has achieved a very much higher asset turnover ratio than Cotton Value, indicating that Engels & Althorpe is able to use its assets far more effectively. It appears that this applies both to fixed assets and stock. Engels & Althorpe also achieves a higher profit on sales, while Cotton Value has suffered a very severe fall in the net profit percentage in the most recent year.

Stock-market opinion may well be concerned at the trends in the profitability and the interest cover for Cotton Value, while the overall superior achievement of Engels & Althorpe is likely to inspire confidence.

Note that share prices at October 1981 may also be affected by post-balance sheet events not covered in the information given.

Key ratios:

	Cotton Value		Engels & Althorpe	
	1981	*1980*	*1981*	*1980*
Liquidity:				
Current ratio	$\dfrac{253}{191} = 1.32$	$\dfrac{232}{168} = 1.38$	$\dfrac{268}{300} = 0.89$	$\dfrac{187}{232} = 0.81$
Acid test	$\dfrac{58}{191} = 0.30$	$\dfrac{37}{168} = 0.22$	$\dfrac{152}{300} = 0.51$	$\dfrac{78}{232} = 0.34$
Capital structure:				
$\dfrac{\text{Total borrowings}}{\text{Total assets}}$	$\dfrac{205}{783} = 26\%$	$\dfrac{180}{745} = 24\%$	$\dfrac{348}{944} = 37\%$	$\dfrac{280}{825} = 34\%$

$\dfrac{\text{Long-term borrowings}}{\text{Long-term funds employed}}$	$\dfrac{14}{592} = 2.5\%$	$\dfrac{12}{577} = 2.1\%$	$\dfrac{48}{644} = 7.4\%$	$\dfrac{48}{593} = 8.1\%$
Total interest cover	$\dfrac{54}{14} = 3.9$	$\dfrac{66}{9} = 7.3$	$\dfrac{193}{12} = 16.1$	$\dfrac{183}{10} = 18.3$

Performance:

Return on equity	$\dfrac{40}{578} = 6.9\%$	$\dfrac{57}{565} = 10.1\%$	$\dfrac{181}{596} = 30.1\%$	$\dfrac{173}{545} = 31.7\%$
Return on total funds	$\dfrac{54}{783} = 6.9\%$	$\dfrac{66}{745} = 8.9\%$	$\dfrac{193}{944} = 20.4\%$	$\dfrac{183}{825} = 22.2\%$
Total asset turnover	$\dfrac{952}{783} = 1.2$	$\dfrac{888}{745} = 1.2$	$\dfrac{1,873}{944} = 2$	$\dfrac{1,668}{825} = 2$
Net profit %	$\dfrac{54}{952} = 5.7\%$	$\dfrac{66}{888} = 7.4\%$	$\dfrac{193}{1,873} = 10.3\%$	$\dfrac{183}{1,668} = 11\%$
Dividend cover	$\dfrac{31}{18} = 1.7$	$\dfrac{41}{18} = 2.3$	$\dfrac{101}{50} = 2$	$\dfrac{93}{45} = 2.1$

Activity ratios:

Fixed asset turnover	$\dfrac{952}{530} = 1.8$	$\dfrac{888}{513} = 1.7$	$\dfrac{1,873}{676} = 2.8$	$\dfrac{1,668}{638} = 2.6$
Stock turnover	$\dfrac{952}{195} = 4.9$	$\dfrac{888}{195} = 4.6$	$\dfrac{1,873}{116} = 16.1$	$\dfrac{1,668}{109} = 15.3$

Investor ratios:

P/E ratio at October 1981	$\dfrac{45}{8.2} = 5.5$	$\dfrac{115}{7.7} = 14.9$
Dividend yield at October 1981	$\dfrac{0.047}{0.45} = 10.5\%$	$\dfrac{0.038}{1.15} = 3.3\%$

Question 22: solution

Silverbridge Working Men's Club

Albert's belief that the accounts present a good picture is open to some question:

(a) Although income has risen, this is partly attributable to the accounting policies chosen rather than successful management. Thus the reducing balance method is used for depreciation, so that the 1989 depreciation charge is down by £5,390 even though exactly the same assets have been used as in 1988.

(b) Repairs in 1988 were £8,000, the year of refurbishment, compared to £500 in 1989. This £7,500 difference would seem to represent the extra costs associated with refurbishment in 1988, and so should not be regarded for analysis purposes as a trading cost of that year. Items (a) and (b) together add up to £12,890 of difference in expense items between 1988 and 1989 that are best excluded for analysis purposes — compared to a £9,290 increase in 1989 income. Thus it is arguable that 1989 saw a £3,600 drop in income achieved.

(c) The gross profit percentage has fallen by 3%. The club's failure to sustain gross profit margins has cost some 3% × £140,000 = £4,200.

(d) Days stock has almost doubled. Tighter stock control policies at the 1988 level would release:

$$\frac{14}{365} \times 98,000 = £3,760$$

(e)   Interest receivable in 1988 presumably came from cash deposits held before paying for the refurbishments. During 1989 new cash balances have built up, but the club has failed to invest these so as to earn interest.

(f)   The 8.3% fall in subscriptions suggests declining support for the club, unless subscription rates have been cut. Increased sales of 7% may reflect a period of closure for refurbishment in 1988 rather than improved trade in 1989.

Thus Albert might well be cautioned against excessive complacency over the 1989 results.

Workings:

	1989	*1988*
Gross profit %	$\dfrac{42,000}{140,000} = 30\%$	$\dfrac{42,900}{130,000} = 33\%$
Wages: sales	$\dfrac{37,200}{140,000} = 27\%$	$\dfrac{35,000}{130,000} = 27\%$
Subscription fall	$\dfrac{100}{1,200} = 8.3\%$	
Sales increase	$\dfrac{10,000}{140,000} = 7\%$	
Days stock	$\dfrac{7,900}{98,000} \times 365 = 29$	$\dfrac{3,520}{87,100} \times 365 = 15$

Question 23: solution

(a)   **Fulke Leisure Group plc — a comparison of the accounts for 19X8 and 19X7:**

Overview:

The company has raised a substantial amount of new long-term finance during the year, from both borrowing and share issue. Most of this money has not yet been used in the business, being held on short-term deposit. Since these deposits account for over 20% of the total assets of the business, the way in which they are employed will have a major effect on the future development of the company.

   If we exclude the effect on the accounts of these short-term deposits the company's profitability has changed little between the two years. There has been some improvement in the profit earned on sales, and some decline in the level of sales generated from assets, but this may well be attributable to an increase in the proportion of sales attributable to hotel activity rather than representing any change in the way either segment of the business is conducted.

Short-term deposits:

The accounts show a substantial increase in short-term deposits, from 1% in 19X7 to 21% in 19X8. This increase would suggest that most of the new long-term finance raised during 19X8 has not yet been invested in the business. The return earned on short-term deposits has fallen during the year, from 10% to 2.7%, but this is probably an indication that the new funds were raised in the latter part of the year rather than indicating any drop in investment performance. In assessing the group's future prospects we need to know how this finance is likely to be used. It might be used to develop one of the current two areas of activity, hotels and brewing, or to develop a new area of activity, or be split between these possibilities. It seems unlikely that these funds will be held on short-term deposit indefinitely, so for the purpose of this report ratios which exclude the impact of these deposits have been computed when considering both liquidity and performance.

Liquidity:

Clearly, while the company continues to hold large cash deposits the liquidity position will be extremely strong. Excluding these deposits, it appears from both the current ratio and the acid test that liquidity has changed little over the year.

Gearing:

Liabilities as a proportion of total funds have changed little over the year. This, together with the fact that the directors have chosen a consistent mix of borrowing and equity to boost long-term funds, suggests that it is the company's policy to maintain a stable level of gearing.

Performance:

The apparent fall of 1.7% of pre-tax return on equity is not particularly significant, in view of the fact that it does appear that the major expansion of equity arising from the new share issue took part in the latter half of the year. Return on total funds, excluding the short-term cash deposits, has changed little. There has, however, been a major change in the way the company earns profit, with a fall in the level of turnover earned from assets and an improvement in the profit earned on sales. This may be attributable to a change in the mix of activities of the group, suggested by the 4% drop in brewery staff and the 7% increase in hotel staff.

Conclusion:

The major question raised by these accounts concerns the directors' plans for using the cash deposits.

Appendix A

Fulke Leisure Group plc: Statement of source and application of funds for the year ended 31 December 19X8

	£000	£000	£000
Sources:			
Profit before tax			19,300
Items not involving movement of funds:			
Depreciation — building		330	
Depreciation — plant		5,700	
Gain on property sale		(500)	
Loss on plant sale		220	
			5,750
Generated from operations			25,050
Other sources:			
Sale of property		1,680	
Sale of plant		580	
Loan		21,385	
Share issue		40,000	
			63,645
			88,695
Applications:			
Purchase of property		20,000	
Purchase of plant		9,000	
Tax paid		5,900	
Dividend paid		4,100	
			39,000
			48,695
Increase/(decrease) in working capital:			
Stock increase		300	
Debtor increase		1,400	
Creditor increase		(1,800)	
Accrual increase		(1,380)	
		(1,480)	
Increase in net liquid funds:			
Deposits	46,500		
Overdrafts	3,680		
Bank	(5)	50,175	48,695

Workings:

Disposals:	*Land & building*	*Plant & fixtures*
Cost	1,200	4,500
Depreciation	20	3,700
Net book value	1,180	800
profit/(loss) on sale	500	(220)
Sale proceeds	1,680	580

Appropriations:	Tax	Dividends
b/fwd	3,500	3,200
P & L	6,500	5,300
	10,000	8,500
c/fwd	4,100	4,400
Cash paid	5,900	4,100

Appendix B

Fulke Leisure Group plc:

	19X8	19X7
Current ratio	$\dfrac{77,820}{36,000} = 2.1$	$\dfrac{29,625}{34,700} = 0.9$
Current ratio excluding short-term deposits	$\dfrac{77,820 - 48,500}{36,000} = 0.8$	$\dfrac{29,625 - 2,000}{34,700} = 0.8$
Acid test	$\dfrac{77,820 - 12,500}{36,000} = 1.8$	$\dfrac{29,625 - 12,200}{34,700} = 0.5$
Acid test excluding short-term deposits	$\dfrac{77,820 - (12,500 + 48,500)}{36,000} = 0.5$	$\dfrac{29,625 - (12,200 + 2,000)}{34,700} = 0.4$
Total liabilities: total funds	$\dfrac{36,000 + 41,820}{36,000 + 41,820 + 157,780} = 33\%$	$\dfrac{34,700 + 18,615}{34,700 + 18,615 + 111,280} = 32\%$
Pre-tax return on equity	$\dfrac{19,300}{157,780} = 12.2\%$	$\dfrac{15,500}{111,280} = 13.9\%$
Return on total operating funds	$\dfrac{20,800}{157,780 + 41,820 + 36,000 - 48,500} = 11.1\%$	$\dfrac{17,600}{111,280 + 18,615 + 34,700 - 2,000} = 10.8\%$
Related: Asset turnover	$\dfrac{171,700}{157,780 + 41,820 + 36,000 - 48,500} = 0.9$	$\dfrac{163,500}{111,280 + 18,615 + 34,700 - 2,000} = 1$
Net profit %	$\dfrac{20,800}{171,700} = 12.1\%$	$\dfrac{17,600}{163,500} = 10.8\%$
Return on short-term deposits	$\dfrac{1,300}{48,500} = 2.7\%$	$\dfrac{17,600}{2,000} = 8.8\%$
Building turnover	$\dfrac{171,700}{117,960} = 1.45$	$\dfrac{163,500}{99,470} = 1.64$
Plant turnover	$\dfrac{171,700}{38,000} = 4.52$	$\dfrac{163,500}{35,500} = 4.60$
Stock turnover	$\dfrac{171,700}{12,500} = 13.74$	$\dfrac{163,500}{12,200} = 13.40$
Debtor turnover	$\dfrac{171,700}{16,700} = 10.28$	$\dfrac{163,500}{15,300} = 10.68$
Short-term deposits as a percentage of total assets	$\dfrac{48,500}{155,960 + 77,820} = 21\%$	$\dfrac{2,000}{134,970 + 2,000} = 1.4\%$

Staff changes:

$$\text{Brewing} \quad \frac{2,500 - 2,600}{2,600} = 4\% \text{ down}$$

$$\text{Hotels} \quad \frac{3,000 - 2,800}{2,800} = 7\% \text{ up}$$

(b) **Extra information:** There are three areas where extra information would be most valuable in analysing these accounts:

(i)   Some indication of the directors' plans for the future use of the cash deposits is needed if you are to predict the future development of the business.

(ii)   A split between the accounts for the brewery division and the hotel division would enable us to gain a much clearer picture of how the business has performed.

(iii) It would also be useful to know when the new loan stock and shares were issued.

Other information which would help us achieve a more thorough analysis includes a breakdown of operating costs, information on asset values, and information about price level movements in both the brewing and hotel industries.

Question 24: solution

(a)   Sales have increased by 30%, more than either distribution costs or administration costs. Since distribution costs tend to contain a higher proportion of variable costs than administration, we would expect these costs to move more in line with sales than the administration costs.

(b)   Stock has increased by less than sales. This is reflected in the 'days stock' ratio:

$$\begin{array}{cc} 1988 & 1987 \\ \dfrac{97}{936} \times 365 = 38 & \dfrac{79}{700} \times 365 = 41 \end{array}$$

Thus the evidence we have points to tighter stock control.

(c)   No new land and buildings have been purchased during the year, the increase being entirely due to revaluation. In fact, therefore, the same land and buildings are now being used to generate 30% more sales.

(d)   Gearing as computed in the question is not comparable between the two years, because the 1988 balance sheet includes the new revaluation reserve of £130m. Had this revaluation applied to 1987 then the gearing ratio for that year would be recomputed:

$$\frac{67 + 200}{210 + 67 + 200 + 130} = 44\%$$

Thus we can see that gearing is in fact unchanged.

Question 25: solution

T plc:

(a)   (i) $\dfrac{167.7 - 2.0}{910} = 18.2\text{p}$

(ii) Weighted average shares:

To $\quad$ 1.4.86 $\quad \dfrac{3}{12} \times 910 \quad = \quad 227.5$

From $\quad$ 1.4.86 $\quad \dfrac{9}{12} \times 1{,}050 = \quad \underline{787.5}$

$$\underline{\underline{1{,}015}}$$

$$\frac{313.1 - 2.0}{1{,}015} = 30.7\text{p}$$

(b) Adjustment: $30.7\text{p} \times \dfrac{2}{3} = 20.4\text{p}$

Question 26: solution

(a) (i) Shareholders:

	1986	1987
Earnings per share (assumes no share issue in 1985/6)	$\dfrac{9{,}520}{39{,}680} = 24\text{p}$	$\dfrac{11{,}660}{39{,}680} = 29.4\text{p}$
Dividend cover	$\dfrac{9{,}520}{2{,}240} = 4.2$	$\dfrac{11{,}660}{2{,}400} = 4.9$

(ii) Trade creditors:

	1986	1987
Creditors turnover	$\dfrac{486{,}300}{32{,}604} = 14.9$	$\dfrac{583{,}900}{37{,}230} = 15.7$
Acid test	$\dfrac{52{,}302}{36{,}862} = 1.4$	$\dfrac{49{,}160}{42{,}475} = 1.2$

(iii) Operating profit: Sales $\quad \dfrac{17{,}238}{486{,}300} = 3.5\% \qquad \dfrac{20{,}670}{583{,}900} = 3.5\%$

Total asset turnover $\quad \dfrac{486{,}300}{36{,}862 + 19{,}840 + 40{,}740} = 5 \qquad \dfrac{583{,}900}{42{,}475 + 19{,}840 + 50{,}000} = 5.2$

(b) Shareholders will be pleased to see improved earnings per share. Although there has been only a modest dividend increase, dividend cover has improved. In view of the high rate of profit retention, they will expect to see continued growth.

Trade creditors will be pleased to see improved creditor turnover, and might usefully compare this with their own experience to see if in fact they are being paid more quickly. They will note the fall in the acid test, and may make a more detailed analysis of the accounts to satisfy themselves on the company's liquidity position.

Internal management will note that they continue to earn the same, rather low, return on sales, while improving slightly on the already high level of sales achieved from assets employed.

Question 27: solution

Nailsea Ltd: Funds flow Statement for the year ended 30 June 1986

	£000	£000
Sources:		
Profit before tax		315
Adjustment for items not involving movement of funds:		
Depreciation		320
Generated from operations		635
Other sources:		
Debentures	300	
Share issue	300	
		600
		1,235
Applications:		
Extraordinary item	75	
Property purchase	400	
Plant purchase	250	
Taxation	110	
Dividend	80	
		915
		320
Increase/(decrease) in working capital:		
Stock increase	175	
Debtor increase	150	
Creditor increase	(60)	
	265	
Bank increase	55	
		320

Ratios:

		1986		1987	
(a)	Return on capital employed*	$\dfrac{342}{2,703 + 300 + 415} = 10\%$		$\dfrac{238}{2,388 + 320} = 8.8\%$	
(b)	Net profit margin	$\dfrac{342}{2,280} = 15\%$		$\dfrac{238}{1,230} = 19.4\%$	
(c)	Asset turnover ratio	$\dfrac{2,280}{2,703 + 300 + 415} = 0.67$		$\dfrac{1,230}{2,388 + 320} = 0.45$	
(d)	Current ratio	$\dfrac{778}{415} = 1.9$		$\dfrac{398}{320} = 1.2$	
(e)	Liquid ratio	$\dfrac{328}{415} = 0.8$		$\dfrac{123}{320} = 0.4$	
(f)	Stock turnover**	$\dfrac{2,280}{450} = 5.1$		$\dfrac{1,230}{275} = 4.5$	

(g)	Days debtors	$\dfrac{250}{2,280} \times 365 = 40$	$\dfrac{100}{1,230} \times 365 = 30$
(h)	Debt : equity	$715 : 2,703 = 0.26 : 1$	$320 : 2,388 = 0.13 : 1$
(i)	Earnings per share***	$\dfrac{175}{1,600} = 10.9\text{p}$	$\dfrac{128}{1,400} = 9.1\text{p}$
(j)	Dividend per share	$\dfrac{85}{1,600} = 5.3\text{p}$	$\dfrac{80}{1,400} = 5.7\text{p}$

* Based on total funds.
** Since cost of sales are not identified, sales are used.
*** Assumes shares issued at full price, not a rights issue.

Comments:

Management have succeeded in boosting the return on total funds employed in the year. This has resulted from a 50% improvement in sales obtained in relation to assets employed, with an erosion of almost a quarter in the net profit margin.

A sales increase of 85% has been supported by increased investment in both fixed assets and working capital, as well as improved asset usage. This investment has been supported both by a new share issue and by raising a long-term loan, thereby increasing the gearing level. These funds, plus those generated from operations, have been adequate to finance expansion and allow for improved liquidity. Stock control has been tightened, but it seems that debtors are taking longer to pay.

The extraordinary item has been excluded from the computation of ratios because it is, by nature, a 'one off'. It would be interesting to know the nature of the 'closure costs' since no plant disposal appears to have been involved.

Shareholders will be pleased to note the improved earnings per share, reflecting the performance achievements we have already noted. They may, however, query the decline in dividend per share, particularly given the improved cash balance.

Question 28: solution

(a) **Blackwell Ltd: Funds flow statement for the year ended 31 December 1986:**

	1986		1985	
	£000	£000	£000	£000
Sources:				
Profit before tax		145		155
Adjustment for item not involving movement of funds:				
Depreciation		105		65
Generated from operations		250		220

Other sources:				
Loan issued	200			
Share issue	100			
	___	300		___
		550		220
Applications:				
Fixed asset purchase	400		—	
Tax paid	50		50	
Dividend paid	40	490	40	90
	___	60	___	130
Increase/(decrease) in working capital:				
Raw material stock increase	5		5	
Manufactured stock increase	60		40	
Debtors increase	40		40	
Trade creditor increase	(20)		(10)	
	___	85	___	75
Cash	(25)		55	
		60		130

(b) The ratios used in the commentaries below are provided in Table 1.

   (i) A small shareholder, seeing a slight fall in dividend per share, lower dividend cover and a substantial fall in earnings per share, is likely to be concerned about the company's performance. A 1.8% decline in return on total funds in 1985 appears to have been attributable to relaxed control over stock and debtors. In 1986 new long-term finance was raised both from borrowing and equity, with substantial new investment in fixed assets. Sales in 1986 only increased by 6.5%, and almost halved in relation to fixed assets employed; combined with further relaxation in working capital control this resulted in a further 6.7% decrease in return on total funds.

      The small shareholder, therefore, is likely to be dissatisfied with the company's management, and certainly reluctant to invest further in this company. Although, as a small shareholder, he or she will have no direct control over management this is likely to lead to complaints at the AGM and receptiveness to any takeover proposition.

  (ii) A trade creditor will be concerned at the drop in the creditor turnover ratio, indicating slower payment by the company. The sluggish trading performance also indicates that this is not a promising customer for expanded sales. However, there is an ample cash balance and no sign of imminent liquidity problems. Providing that the supplier can afford to accept some delay in payment then this company would be accepted as a customer, but would probably be sold goods at prices which reflect the extra credit to be given. The creditor would be wise to review this account regularly (say once a year) to see if the company does hit problems.

Table 1

Ratio	1986	1985	1984
Acid test	$\dfrac{290}{185} = 1.6$	$\dfrac{275}{160} = 1.7$	$\dfrac{180}{150} = 1.2$
Gearing	$\dfrac{185 + 200}{185 + 200 + 695} = 36\%$	$\dfrac{160}{160 + 545} = 23\%$	$\dfrac{150}{150 + 480} = 24\%$
Pre-tax on equity	$\dfrac{145}{695} = 20.9\%$	$\dfrac{155}{545} = 28.4\%$	$\dfrac{150}{480} = 31.2\%$
Return on total funds	$\dfrac{165}{185 + 200 + 695} = 15.3\%$	$\dfrac{155}{160 + 545} = 22\%$	$\dfrac{150}{150 + 480} = 23.8\%$
Related:			
Asset turnover	$\dfrac{660}{185 + 200 + 695} = 0.6$	$\dfrac{620}{160 + 545} = 0.9$	$\dfrac{600}{150 + 480} = 1$
Net profit %	$\dfrac{165}{660} = 25\%$	$\dfrac{155}{620} = 25\%$	$\dfrac{150}{600} = 25\%$
Stock turnover	$\dfrac{330}{200} = 1.6$	$\dfrac{300}{135} = 2.2$	$\dfrac{300}{90} = 3.3$
Days debtors	$\dfrac{160}{660} \times 365 = 88$	$\dfrac{120}{620} \times 365 = 71$	$\dfrac{80}{600} \times 365 = 49$
Creditor turnover	$\dfrac{660}{90} = 7.3$	$\dfrac{620}{70} = 8.9$	$\dfrac{600}{60} = 10$
Fixed asset turnover	$\dfrac{660}{590} = 1.1$	$\dfrac{620}{295} = 2.1$	$\dfrac{600}{360} = 1.7$
Sales increase	$\dfrac{40}{620} = 6.5\%$	$\dfrac{20}{600} = 3.3\%$	
Earnings per share	$\dfrac{95}{350} = 27.1p$	$\dfrac{105}{300} = 35p$	$\dfrac{100}{300} = 33.3p$
Dividend per share	$\dfrac{45}{350} = 12.9p$	$\dfrac{40}{300} = 13.3p$	$\dfrac{40}{100} = 13.3p$
Dividend cover	$\dfrac{95}{45} = 2.1$	$\dfrac{105}{40} = 2.6$	$\dfrac{100}{40} = 2.5$

Question 29: solution

Comparison of G plc and H plc:

Overview:
G plc is considerably weaker than H plc in terms both of liquidity and performance. H plc has accumulated substantial cash balances, to the point where a quarter of its total assets are invested outside the business.

Liquidity:
G's current ratio and acid test seem alarmingly low, although we should be cautious about comparison with a company that holds such substantial cash balances as H. Both companies take similar periods of trade credit, suggesting that G plc has not got a problem in meeting obligations. The lower days stock and days debtors ratios for H suggest that G has some

opportunity to improve liquidity by tighter working capital control. It would be interesting to know what plans G has for refinancing the debentures repayable in the coming year.

Performance:
G achieves little more than half the return on trading assets compared to H. This is attributable to the low return earned on sales. Although both companies earn a similar gross profit percentage, other expenses as a proportion of sales are 10% higher for G. At first sight G would seem to have a more economical distribution arrangement but a vastly more costly administration. However, this difference may well be attributable to differences in the way in which the two companies allocate expenses.

Investment:
We have already observed that the directors of H have accumulated cash for investment amounting to some 25%. With a dividend cover ratio of 3, compared to G's 2, there is clearly a policy of retaining profits for investment by the company. The return earned on investment in fact is not much below the return earned on operating assets. Unless there are plans to employ these funds in expanding trading activities, it would appear that H is moving gradually towards becoming as much an investment company as a brewery.

Conclusion:
These two companies are dramatically different in their financial position. G seems to have problems of controlling administrative costs as well as working capital. H has a tightly run trading operation and appears to be using the funds generated from that to build up an investment company.

Ratios:

	G plc	H plc
Current ratio	$\dfrac{77,000}{144,900} = 0.5$	$\dfrac{10,580}{2,810} = 3.8$
Acid test	$\dfrac{41,000}{144,900} = 0.3$	$\dfrac{9,880}{2,810} = 3.5$
Gearing	$\dfrac{144,900 + 68,000}{144,900 + 68,000 + 336,100} = 39\%$	$\dfrac{2,810}{2,810 + 22,070} = 11\%$
Post-tax return on equity	$\dfrac{13,310}{336,100} = 4\%$	$\dfrac{1,770}{22,070} = 8\%$
Post-tax return on equity	$\dfrac{20,810}{336,100} = 6.2\%$	$\dfrac{2,970}{22,070} = 13.5\%$
Return on total funds	$\dfrac{34,510}{144,900 + 68,000 + 336,100} = 6.3\%$	$\dfrac{2,970}{2,810 + 22,070} = 11.9\%$
Return on trading assets*	N/A	$\dfrac{2,200}{17,940} = 12.3\%$
Secondary ratios:		
Asset turnover	$\dfrac{387,400}{144,900 + 68,000 + 336,100} = 0.7$	$\dfrac{11,500}{17,940} = 0.6$
Net profit %	$\dfrac{34,510}{387,400} = 9\%$	$\dfrac{2,200}{11,500} = 19\%$

Gross profit %	$\dfrac{183,000}{387,400} = 47\%$	$\dfrac{5,400}{11,500} = 47\%$
Distribution : sales	$\dfrac{12,200}{387,400} = 3\%$	$\dfrac{1,930}{11,500} = 17\%$
Administration : Sales	$\dfrac{136,400}{387,400} = 35\%$	$\dfrac{1,270}{11,500} = 11\%$
Return on investments	—	$\dfrac{770}{6,940} = 11\%$
Days stock	$\dfrac{36,000}{204,400} \times 365 = 64$	$\dfrac{700}{6,100} \times 365 = 42$
Days debtors	$\dfrac{25,000}{387,400} \times 365 = 24$	$\dfrac{410}{11,500} \times 365 = 13$
Creditors turnover	$\dfrac{387,400}{39,800} = 9.7$	$\dfrac{6,100}{600} = 10.2$
Dividend cover	$\dfrac{133,100}{6,500} = 2$	$\dfrac{1,770}{600} = 3$

* H plc holds 28% of total assets in the form of cash, and receives 25% of pre-tax income from investments. Therefore a separate return on trading asset ratio has been computed for H plc, and secondary ratios have been based thereon. G plc holds only 1% of total assets as cash, so that separate analysis is not considered necessary.

Question 30: solution

(a)

		Easthope	Quilter
(i)	Funds generated from operations (net profit + depreciation)	£170,000	£250,000
(ii)	Proprietorship ratio	$\dfrac{600}{860} = 70\%$	$\dfrac{900}{1,200} = 75\%$
(iii)	Working capital ratio	$\dfrac{455}{260} = 1.75$	$\dfrac{525}{300} = 1.75$
(iv)	Net profit : sales	$\dfrac{120}{2,050} = 5.9\%$	$\dfrac{130}{2,620} = 5\%$
(v)	Return on equity	$\dfrac{120}{600} = 20\%$	$\dfrac{130}{900} = 14.4\%$

(b) Quilter has a stronger cash flow from trading and a slightly lower level of gearing, giving more capacity to sustain extra borrowing. Easthope, on the other hand, trades more profitably, achieving a better profit margin on sales and a substantially higher return on equity.

(c) From a lending point of view we are concerned with the ability of the company to meet the deadlines for repayment, and the margin of security in the event of default. Quilter seems more attractive because:

(i)   Since profits are to be paid out as dividends spare cash flows
       from trading arise only from depreciation which is higher for
       Quilter.
(ii)   Quilter is marginally lower geared.
(iii) Quilter's premises offer an attractive prospect for security.

Question 31: solution

Overview:
Although these two companies are said to be in the same industry, they do
business in very different ways. Skin plc is the stronger performer, and also
has safer levels of liquidity and gearing.

Liquidity and gearing:
The current ratio shows Skin plc as having a somewhat stronger liquidity
position, while the acid test shows Skin as very substantially stronger.
Bone's gearing, with over 70% of total assets financed by liabilities, is also
very much higher than Skin's. This involves a high degree of risk for Bone,
but does benefit shareholders by boosting a low return on total funds (less
than half of Skin's at 0.8%) to a pre-tax return on equity of 24%, close to
Skin's 26.4%.

Performance:
As we have seen, Bone's pre-tax return on total funds is less than half
Skin's. Compared with Skin, Bone achieves almost three times the level of
sales in relation to assets employed, but achieves less than ⅕ of the profit
in relation to sales. Looking at Skin's high gross profit percentage and low
fixed asset turnover suggests that Skin may be primarily engaged in manufacturing and Bone primarily in wholesaling or retailing.

Conclusion:
From our analysis Skin appears as a better performer, and also as more
financially sound. However, our analysis of performance suggests that the
two companies are engaged in such dramatically different aspects of their
business as not to be comparable. In particular, Bone's high current
liabilities may be attributable to trading pattern rather than deliberate
borrowing so that return on equity might offer a better basis for performance comparison.

Key ratios:

	Skin	Bone
Current ratio	$\dfrac{185}{154} = 1.2$	$\dfrac{190}{170} = 1.1$
Acid test	$\dfrac{139}{154} = 0.9$	$\dfrac{80}{170} = 0.8$
Days stock	$\dfrac{46}{775} \times 365 = 22$	$\dfrac{110}{1{,}380} \times 365 = 29$
Days debtors	$\dfrac{124}{1{,}020} \times 365 = 44$	$\dfrac{70}{1{,}500} \times 365 = 17$

Total liabilities : total assets	$\dfrac{154 + 25}{154 + 25 + 277} = 39\%$	$\dfrac{170 + 10}{170 + 10 + 75} = 71\%$
Post-tax return on equity	$\dfrac{50}{277} = 18.1\%$	$\dfrac{11}{75} = 14.7\%$
Pre-tax return on equity	$\dfrac{73}{277} = 26.4\%$	$\dfrac{18}{75} = 24\%$
Pre-tax return on total funds	$\dfrac{75}{154 + 25 + 277} = 16.4\%$	$\dfrac{20}{170 + 10 + 75} = 7.8\%$
Asset turnover	$\dfrac{1,020}{154 + 25 + 277} = 2.2$	$\dfrac{1500}{170 + 10 + 75} = 5.9\%$
Net profit %	$\dfrac{75}{1,020} = 7.4\%$	$\dfrac{20}{1,500} = 1.3\%$
Gross profit %	$\dfrac{245}{1,020} \doteqdot 24\%$	$\dfrac{120}{1,500} = 8\%$
Distribution : sales	$\dfrac{120}{1,020} = 11.8\%$	$\dfrac{40}{1,500} = 2.7\%$
Administration : sales	$\dfrac{50}{1,020} = 5\%$	$\dfrac{60}{1,500} = 4\%$
Fixed asset turnover	$\dfrac{1,020}{271} = 3.8$	$\dfrac{1,500}{65} = 23$

Question 32: solution

The company has expanded substantially during 1988, while at the same time managing to achieve an increase of over a third in the return on total funds achieved. This is largely attributable to an improved net profit margin. This appears to have been achieved by accepting a lower gross profit margin, perhaps to help achieve the sales increase, and a tight control over expenses which have not risen in line with sales. However, it would be useful to check that there has not been any reallocation of costs from the 'cost of sales' category to the 'expenses' category in 1988.

Liquidity has fallen, although there is still a substantial cash balance. The drop in creditors turnover suggests that the company might be straining the patience of suppliers in order to finance expansion.

Ratios:

	1986		1987	
Liquidity ratio	$\dfrac{426,532}{77,571} = 5.5$		$\dfrac{451,286}{145,308} = 3.1$	
Return on total funds	$\dfrac{150,794}{649,095 + 77,571} = 20.8\%$		$\dfrac{267,096}{822,707 + 145,308} = 27.6\%$	
Asset turnover	$\dfrac{2,154,203}{649,095 + 77,571} = 3$		$\dfrac{3,196,124}{822,707 + 145,308} = 3.3$	

Net profit %	$\dfrac{150,794}{2,154,203} = 7\%$	$\dfrac{267,076}{3,196,124} = 8.4\%$
Gross profit %	$\dfrac{732,429}{2,154,203} = 34\%$	$\dfrac{894,915}{3,196,124} = 28\%$
Expenses : sales	$\dfrac{581,635}{2,154,203} = 27\%$	$\dfrac{627,819}{3,196,124} = 19.6\%$
Creditors turnover	$\dfrac{2,154,203}{77,571} = 27.8$	$\dfrac{3,196,124}{145,308} = 22$

Tutorial note:
The scope of the answer has been deliberately restricted in view of the indication given by the examiner in specifying a minimum of five ratios.

Index

Acid Test 7
Asset turnover 26, 27, 29

Capital gearing 13
Common size statement 40
Companies Act 1985 2, 8
Comparative data 3–5
Creditors turnover 11
Current ratio 7

Days creditors 10–11
Days debtors 10
Days stock 9–10
Debt, equity ratio 16
Deferred taxation 25, 52
Degree of capital gearing 14–15, 18
Dividend cover 37
Dividend yield 36

Earnings per share (EPS) 31–7

Financial leverage 13
Funds flow statements 40–1

Gearing 13–21
Gross Profit % 27–8

Inflation, impact on accounts 2
Interest cover 17, 18
Investor ratios 31–7

Leasing 19–20
Leverage 13
Limitations of ratio analysis 1–2, 3

Liquidity 7–12
Liquidity ratio 7

Market share 29–30
Multivariate analysis 41

Net profit % 26–9

'Off Balance Sheet' finance 19–20
Operational gearing 20

Preference shares 16
Price earnings ratio (P/E) 36
Primary ratio 23

Quick asset ratio 7

Ratio analysis, defined and discussed 3
Return on capital employed (ROCE) 4,
   23–6

Secondary ratios 26–29
Solvency 7
Statements of standard accounting
   practice (SSAP's) 1
Stock turnover 9

Taxation 25
Trend statements 39–40

Users (of accounts) 1

Working capital activity ratios 8–11